Introduction

Developing riches takes tenacious purpose, willpower, regularity, and patience. It additionally takes a deep dedication to researching and fully comprehending your financial investment and also its threats.

An example of this frame of mind comes from one of my preferred tales showing the nature of wealth and also exactly how we operate in the present to safeguard the future, both for ourselves and for the future generation. Tony Deden, of Edelweiss Holdings, thinks his job as handling household possessions implies, most importantly securing capital. He tells of fulfilling a date farmer who inherited an orchard of almost a thousand trees. As they're touring the grounds, Mr. Deden sees a hundred brand-new trees that have actually just recently been grown. He asks the owner how long it will consider the newly grown trees to bear fruit.

" Virtually 20 years for the trees to be effective," clarifies the farmer, "but market top quality fruit will not be generated for another two decades after that."

This is sensational to Western ears. Why would a man invest in something where he will never get any kind of incentive? Why would a guy do this? The farmer starts revealing Deden photos of his excellent grandpa, his grandfather and his dad. And then he claims something that will show so crucial to us as we relocate via this book - the orchard proprietor states he's merely a steward. He is a caretaker of this orchard as well as future generations will certainly do the exact same. In this man's world view, this is what wealth means - a responsibility to our families and the treatment of what has actually been offered for us to handle, except ourselves, yet eventually for others.

I enjoy the US and also Americans. I enjoy the American spirit of ahead thinking and I have found a honesty in the people right here that I have not experienced anywhere else in the world. But this old method of thinking of wealth is mainly lacking from Americans' mind. I would humbly recommend that it is very beneficial to consider this old mindset.

Comprehending ourselves as guardians rather than owners has the ability to entirely alter how we reside in this globe and care for those we like. We are below for just a minute in the scheme of points as well as due to that, we are a lot more caretakers than owners. It's our obligation to manage well what we have actually been honored with in this life.

What are these concepts carrying out in a book concerning Asian rugs? The solution is extra direct and basic than it appears initially appearance; the collection, care and security of Asian rugs provides a superb framework to explore the better principles behind value, wealth and also riches preservation. Making use of my experience as both an Asian rug broker and also collector, this book will attempt to illuminate wider ideas on how to identify value, how to preserve and safeguard your wealth with Oriental carpets. This publication is a little bit uncommon in that it is not just regarding handmade Asian carpets and also what is important to comprehend regarding them, but basically it is also regarding generational riches as well as exactly how to consider, spend for, and also construct tradition.

Beginning

I have actually remained in the Asian rug company for over 40 years. I was born in Iran and also came to the United States in 1976 to go to university, right before the major routine adjustment of this period. This changed my life in a way I might have never ever envisioned when I left my home nation. Because my daddy was no more able to send cash abroad for my tuition, I had to leave institution as well as needed a way to earn money. I have actually always been independent and when I left school, I determined that as opposed to trying to help somebody else, I 'd see what I could do on my own.

I have an approach of work that I've consistently complied with, and that is if you do what you really enjoy, you will unavoidably flourish. This is something my daddy opened my mind to, that it's the greatest gift to get up in the morning delighted to head to function. If you love what you do everyday, you currently have wealth beyond action.

This is why I chose the carpet business; I enjoy Oriental rugs. I essentially matured with them. My daddy was a collection agency and his friend remained in the rug profession. At any time he obtained an exquisite piece, my father insisted on being the very first to see it. I matured with several of the finest carpets I have actually ever seen in all my years in the business, as a child in my own home. My papa's admiration for extraordinary, superb home furnishings and also care in exactly how he designated our home is exactly how I discovered quality, individuality as well as appeal.

My mother, her 2 sis and my granny, were all rugmakers. Something not popular to people in the United States, is that many people in Iran make rugs, as a hobby. In a comparable way, United States craftspeople make gorgeous, local quilts. Each town, city or people has its own design of rug and also many individuals make them, some expertly as well as some, like the ladies in my family members, as a creative activity, normally providing the rugs away as presents to others in the family members. As a kid I liked being with the females as they made these items, as well as I had fun with the wool they made use of, simply to be around them. When I was 5 years old, they educated me how to make a knot, among the thousands that go into a handmade, distinctive, Asian carpet.

Once I found out exactly how to make the rugs myself, I would certainly see carpets in other peoples' homes as well as I valued them in a much deeper method, due to the fact that I understood the construction of them. I can consider a knot and also recognize from the means it was tied, based upon the round back of the knot, what kind of weaving method was utilized. I can instantly acknowledge if a carpet was wool, silk or a combination of both. At the very same time I began to end up being attuned to gathering since my daddy expanded to be a collection agency. Between recognizing how to make rugs and my daddy's curation of the splendid things he brought right into our residence, I began to have some discernment. At a really young age, I could recognize what top quality and appeal were, especially in carpets.

Something else that lots of people in the United States do not recognize concerning Iran; everyone has carpets. They are utilized the means wall-to-wall carpeting is used below. In Iran, hand-made rugs are not simply for huge, elaborately decorated houses. The simplest person with the most small life will have rugs. So regardless of where I went when I was growing up, I saw rugs, recognized them, and also studied them.

When I recognized that I was mosting likely to have to quit university to earn money, I chose I would choose the carpet trade. Due to my youth experience making carpets, and also my daddy's remarkable taste, I understood just how to recognize quality as well as uniqueness in a carpet when I saw one, yet I really did not always understand just how to price it. Due to the fact that I really did not completely recognize the market (as well as also due to the fact that I had less than $2,000 to my name), rather than beginning with a shop, I started in this company by going to public auctions. I would buy carpets at public auction, as well as because I found out how to do great repairs on carpets growing up, I might fix a low cost damaged rug to the factor where the repair was invisible as well as offer it to a New york city wholesaler or one more customer. The very first five years I was in business, this is exactly how I made my living, by going to auctions, repairing and also marketing rugs. I learned a lot in that time, it was really an education by fire as well as I did get melted.

While I was working making ends meet for my family members, I had not been really doing what I intended to do, which was to have an appropriate store of my very own. At the very same time, I knew I had not been ready. Also simply buying, fixing and also marketing rugs from public auctions, I made various mistakes. I simply didn't have the knowledge I needed to appropriately, consistently review the rates of a rug. I bought a carpet in an auction that I paid $3600 in Chicago. I believed it was a Sarouk, but it ended up being a Sparta (Turkish) which is not nearly as great. It was 11' X 17'. Completions and also sides needed job as well as moth damages that required to be reknotted. I worked with it for about a week and also wound up marketing it for concerning $1500. I lost a few of my funding and all of my time. I thought I would certainly be able to market it for $7000 - $8000. Two dealers looked at the rug and also informed me that it was a Sparta. "Are you sure?" They were sure, so I marketed it to them.

That was a difficult experience as well as it had not been the only one, sadly not by a longshot. I have actually purchased a lot of rugs I should not have, as well as I have actually lost a lot of money and time. But I securely believe these "poor" experiences are an essential part of the individual I am today. It took making a great deal of blunders with value and also rates, but I eventually involved a deep understanding of top quality and the asian rug market. We tend to be so afraid to make a mistake, and also specifically to shed money. The best choice I made was not to have a store before I was ready. Without needing to sustain a whole shop, I could offer myself the moment I required to discover the market, and make blunders without bankrupting myself. Without these "negative" experiences, I would not have learned what I know and also I wouldn't have actually learned as quickly as I did, and also I never would have discovered what I required to be effective.

Another time a supplier from LA was preparing to visit my store in Louisville.

This was the first time I would certainly ever collaborated with him. He was available in and suched as 2 carpets. One, a serapi, had an area in the middle that was completely torn out and missing. The other rug, a Zigler Mahal, required small fixing. That I was going to market retail. The dealership asked just how much I wanted and also I asked how much he would pay. He said $36,000, as well as I claimed "ok!" I had been planning on offering them for $24,000, and I had actually paid about $5,700 for them. Right now, I still didn't totally understand the carpet market, however it exercised in my favor.

When I started to understand a little concerning the marketplace, I did much better. This is something else that I assume we ignore; sometimes, it just takes a little enhancement in ability to see a huge renovation in outcome. At one auction particularly I snooped a beautiful carpet that required some small repair service. I had the ability to purchase it for $1,700, do the repair services utilizing the abilities I gained from my grandmother and also mom, as well as sell the carpet for a fair market price of $25,000. This isn't the type of offer you will find on a daily basis, obviously, however without the experience of buying and offering the incorrect rugs, I never would have acknowledged that chance when it came.

As you start your very own venture right into collecting, you will certainly locate that you have what feels like a boundless variety of carpets to select from - this is both incredibly delightful as well as at the same time can seem very challenging. There are rugs from different nations, and also excavating much deeper, various cities and various people. You will find city rugs, village carpets as well as tribal rugs, having different qualities, designs, signs and also products. I promise you, as you use several of the basic concepts I lay out in this book, you will have the discernment as well as expertise to be able to maneuver this huge market.

You will additionally find various specific niches or sort of carpets to concentrate on if you want. There are piled rugs (the most usual), kilim carpets (carpets made in only the level weave that binds completions of a heap rug), prayer rugs, salt bags, saddle bags as well as tent bags, to call a handful. Serapis, which were originally utilized to wrap various other rugs for transportation, are now one of the rarest, most treasured, as well as most costly of any kind of antique rug on the market. Concentrating on a particular niche or an area - or both - will enable you to deeply study the background of your carpets. Discovering the people, places and also history of these carpets is a joy that improves the experience of owning them in a manner that is immeasurable and also can make the carpets, in regards to their worth to you, practically invaluable.

My preferred clients are collectors. I love when someone not only finds out about carpets however is as excited as I am about having them. I've constantly tried to educate my clients who wish to discover, and I think of myself as more an instructor than a vendor. I came to comprehend with my own experience with the rug market, when you begin to find out also a little regarding the rugs - it does not have to be every little thing - you begin to discover well valued quality rugs. If you just go and also speak with a good rug supplier, you will discover the fundamentals. Go and also speak with every one of them in the area as well as when you're traveling, you'll find the appropriate fit. But you need to do the leg work, you have to go into a shop, ask questions concerning the rugs, take a look at them as well as touch them. Lay a carpet out, flip it over, walk on it. Walk around it as well as observe how the shades alter as you move the carpet. Ask to take it house and deal with it for a day. It will certainly inform you points. You will begin to see the differences in the rugs. Then acquire a rug that you like, that's handmade. This is just how you will certainly begin. You aren't mosting likely to know every little thing concerning carpets the very first time you buy one, that would be impossible. But you will certainly never ever know anything concerning them up until you begin engaging with them. As soon as you begin to communicate with the rugs, you will begin to recognize enough to begin seeing worth. Like all points in this life, it's a procedure as well as a journey.

With this publication I want to instruct you a little concerning what I learned from being in the business for 40 years. I am certain that after reading it, you will certainly know sufficient to seem like you can start as well as will certainly have built the confidence to start gathering your very own rugs.

The Fundamentals

Oriental carpets have been and also remain to be stores of wide range for as lengthy as gold has actually been utilized. Numerous routines and federal governments have come and gone as well as with them their fiat money. Asian rugs have been a way to protect riches as well as purchasing power, making it through great financial and financial modifications as well as wars as well as political chaos that we human beings remain to cause on ourselves. Political discontent is as old as capitals as well as sometimes we require to gather our points, roll up a rug, accumulate our loved ones and also flee to survive the turmoil. Genuine Asian rugs permit us to not only have a touch of elegance in our every day lives but additionally quietly expand our generational wealth with mobility as well as utility.

People have a tendency to think about wide range mostly as just how much of a specific currency somebody has, and also we like to distill it to a number. I would certainly state that this isn't all that helpful over time and is a diversion from the worth that is concealed in that number. To climb right into a vintage car as well as bring the engine to life or to taste the subtleties as well as splendor of long aged red wine or walk with bare feet throughout an antique Lilihan rug defies distilling our wide range right into a solitary number denominated in an ever-declining currency. A remarkable point about hand-crafted carpets is that owning one is really accessible for the majority of people, virtually no matter means. Presently, a tiny genuine carpet of beautiful building and high quality can be bought for just a few hundred dollars, occasionally just $150. Some people in the United States will certainly need to save lengthy and also hard for that, but it is possible. This is why I like these rugs, and also this nation.

What makes a rug "collectable?".

In my experience offering carpets, most people do not start with the suggestion of starting a collection, however rather the desire to possess even more rugs is kindled with that very first purchase. I believe that if you are considering acquiring asian rugs, and you are reading this book, you will certainly wind up being some kind of an enthusiast therefore it will be helpful upfront to define what is worth accumulating and what is, at the end of the day, "simply a rug." What I call a "actual" carpet, provided correct care, will always raise in value in time. These "actual" carpets have 3 very certain high qualities which trigger this increase - the carpet needs to be just one of a kind, handmade, and should be from one of 4 rug making nations. There are constantly exemptions certainly, however as you begin on the road to finding out about collecting and buying carpets that have all 3 of these high qualities, you should rest assured that you will have at least a degree of success in investing.

One of a kind carpets.

Handmade Asian rugs are unique, among kind productions of charm. They are the expression of a string of craftsmens; the pattern maker that visualizes the style. The color maker who blends and develops the shades for the wool. The weavers that hand knot the rug. The shearers who shape the woven wool to reveal the last pattern as well as elegance of the rug. And finally you, the proprietor, that produces a space for these masterpieces to influence and enrich your day-to-day live. Presenting them to showcase their singular, sublime elegance is a type of reverence.

Possessing a handmade Asian carpet is a fantastic obligation as well as success. We are curators as well as caretakers of these prizes, preserving them for future generations..

This awareness becomes an increasing number of critical as the forces of globalization and also technology remove the old craft of carpet production. These items are truly, actually one of a kind. No handmade carpet can be recreated. Pairs of small rugs are made sometimes, yet they are still unique, also to one another when thoroughly analyzed.

Due to the fact that these rugs are among a kind, accumulating them offers you ownership of something no person else worldwide has. I like to inform my enthusiast clients that having a "genuine" carpet resembles possessing a "actual" Picasso - it's a real artwork that you can stroll on.

Handmade

The following aspect of credibility for an Oriental rug is that it is handmade. Carpet production is an old craft that has actually been given with a lot of generations it's almost impossible to follow it back to its starts. Rugs have actually been woven for kings, tsars and also emperors. And also rugs have actually been woven for the most modest of families, often by the rugmaker because household. Each knot is connected by hand, each thread is clipped by hand or sheared by hand. The structure of the rugs, also the looms are constructed by hand. The variation triggered by the fundamentally hand-made nature of these pieces is a major part of what contributes to their uniqueness, which gives worth.

The transmission of the craft of handmade woven carpets from generation to generation is being damaged by the march of innovation, and as a consequence these carpets are yearly becoming extra rare. As even more young people most likely to university, and to the cities to locate help their households, the ancient abilities come to be much less understood. The rug market is presently well provided no doubt, yet an increasing number of the marketplace is comprised of manufacturing facility made carpets and also less and fewer are handcrafted with the skill and understanding of generations disappearing. Theirs is an one-of-a-kind, inexpressible charm emitting and disclosing itself as a handmade rug will do. Industrial manufacturing facility carpets do not have these top qualities. This belongs to the reason well made, well took care of and also gorgeous handcrafted carpets increase each year in value. As a piece ages it ends up being better and will last for generations. I like to think of these as a means of protecting generational wide range but far better than money or digital figures on a bank declaration. These are points of outstanding charm that are wide range not only for our daily enjoyment however beauty as wide range that can be handed down to future generations. Affluent households are known to have carpets that have been in the family members for generations and also they age magnificently, retaining their splendor and magic..

The four rug making countries

There are a plethora of nations that generate carpets, but just four generate what I describe as "genuine" rugs; the carpets created in these locations are of a quality that is unrivaled by any kind of others. I want to aid you obtain familiar and also comfy with these countries as well as the type of carpets they produce.

In addition to there being 4 countries that develop Asian rugs, there are 3 various "kinds" of rug within each country. "City" rugs are made by weavers with sophisticated skills, access to a panoply of materials as well as dyes as well as usually feature intricate patterns that are curvelinar. "Town" carpets are less complicated in design, normally made in a family members home and also while they might include some curvilinear aspects, they are mostly geometric in their patterns. "Tribal" carpets are the most basic in pattern, always geometric, as well as usually uneven in shape because they are made by nomadic tribal people as well as their impend stress will certainly change as they evacuate a partially ended up rug to proceed to their next place.

Iran

Let's begin with among the biggest manufacturers of Asian rugs, as well as naturally, the country I come from. Iran has a long background of producing some of the finest rugs in the world, as well as to this day, it still has some of the most experienced and imaginative pattern manufacturers and weavers to be located anywhere. There are actually thousands of various sort of carpets from Iran, a lot of to consist of right here. Rather, here is a list of a few of my favored kinds of carpets as well as their features.

Tabriz:

A really great city carpet, commonly including elaborate flower style and also a facility medallion. Tabriz carpets are largely and firmly woven. This city has actually generated a few of the most renowned masters of the craft in the 19th century.

Ghom:
A very premium city rug, Ghoms are made from silk or Kork woollen (wool spun from the first shearing of wool off the neck of a child lamb) as well as carefully knotted. They include the a lot more complicated curvilinear layouts of city carpets.

Hamadan:
A village rug that includes fantastic and deep colors such as cobalt and scarlet. The Hamadan pattern is a satisfying mix of the sophisticated curvilinear city design and also the tribal geometric.

Heriz:
One more town rug, known for beautiful veggie dye tinting. In Heriz rugs you will certainly find some of the best instances of the blending of sophisticated curvilinear city-style patterns and also strong tribal-style geometric style.

Baluch:
A tribal rug frequently including a repeating geometric pattern and in a darker shade combination of browns, dark blues as well as also black. Since these rugs are made by wanderers, they tend to be quite little for mobility. The square size, generally difficult to find in Oriental carpets, is much more common in Baluch.

Gabbeh:
Made by a number of different people, a Gabbeh is absolutely a nomadic design of carpet. Woollen string is generally hand spun from the tribe's very own sheep, and also includes extremely simple layouts. No patterns are used developing these carpets, it's all from the weaver's imagination.

Previous Soviet Union
The previous Soviet Union has a number of regions that produce exquisite handmade rugs that are really deserving of gathering. While Iranian carpets, especially city-produced, can often tend toward complicated as well as rich patterns as well as shades, numerous carpets from this area will have brighter shades as well as bolder, a lot more geometric styles.

Caucasian:
These are different and also commonly complex rugs woven by the areas on either side of the Caucasus Hills. Patterns and color can differ greatly based upon location however still be considered "White." Similarly, the weaving can vary from great to coarse, depending upon where a carpet is made. The attractive aspects in the carpet variety from geometric to curvilinear, straightforward to complicated.

Kazak:
These rugs are still plentifully made in the Caucasus region. These carpets are brilliantly tinted and also feature layouts that are strikingly geometric. The area is primarily Armenian and nomadic Kurds. The rugs are normally little, commonly with celebrities (8 sharp) or crabs and other geometric forms in repeating patterns. Antique Kazaks in good condition rival antique Persian rugs for charm and also value.

Turkoman:
These rugs are excellent instances of the "all over" style pattern. This region is known for the Bokhara design. Bokhara carpets are really traded in Bokhara rather than being made there. The tribes that make these carpets are singular and personal individuals, typically not desiring others in the areas they live in. Each tribe has their own "Gul," an octagonal pattern that looks like an elephant's impact.

Baluchi:
The Baluchi are people that travel via the Turkoman region. These carpets mirror the tribal lives of individuals that produce them. They are less great, but no much less gorgeous than city rugs. They can be irregular fit because of the horizontal looms they are woven on, as well as because they are commonly relocated from place to place while being woven.

Soumak (Sumak):.
Soumak is a Caucasus area and words "Soumak" refers more to a design of weaving than a specific layout. A Soumak is a level weave that is more resilient than the flat-weave of the Kilim. The Soumak strategy covers colored weft yarns over as well as under the warp, compelling the threads to rise from the rug, making something that looks a great deal like needlework

and does not have the holes or slits that can be seen in a kilim weave. These carpets usually have a simpler, geometric tribal-style pattern to them. Real antique Soumaks are rare.

Afghanistan.

Rugs made in Afghanistan are tribal in style as well as layout, mirroring the nomadic life of the people there. This is also an overwhelmingly muslim country, with the rug patterns sticking to the concepts of geometric design just, as opposed to allowing people or pets to be shown. The carpets are mainly red, black as well as cream color, and will certainly often include eco-friendlies. Much of the pieces will consist of the octagonal "elephants foot" pattern as the area of the rug, with a boundary of smaller sized octagonal "feet" around the side of the rug.

As much of these weavings are done for use in a nomadic life, there is quite a range in the type of woven items one can find from this location, other than carpets. These consist of bags, saddle decors, fancy "door surrounds" that would certainly embellish the opening of a tent, as well as smaller sized "rugs" that are not planned for the flooring, yet rather to hang over a camping tent opening or on a wall, both for improvement as well as insulation. And also obviously, prayer carpets. The carpets of this area have a tendency to be densely woven, heavy and extremely tough.

Turkey.

Turkish Asian carpets were amongst a few of the initial to be exported to the west, and subsequently, several of one of the most valued rugs in Europe and also the US. Turkey historically is a rigorous Muslim country and as such, includes elegant design as well as patterns as accurate depictions of point from the environment, whether people, plants or animals, is prohibited.

Bergama:.

It's thought that Bergama carpets have actually been made because the 11th century. These rugs can be geometric or curvalinear in pattern, are generally constructed from wool pile and also are normally rather roughly woven. Their patterns, nonetheless, are typically complicated and fairly attractive, making them equally as magnificent as rugs with a high knot matter.

Hereke:.

Among the better-known styles of rug, the Hereke rugs feature fine curvilinear patterns in the highest tradition of Asian carpets. Hereke is also known for making bigger carpets, and also at once were the unique choice of emperors. While much of Turkey's rug designs are less sophisticated than other areas, Hereke carpets are especially valued for the fineness of their design.

Oushak:.

These rugs are presently highly treasured in the west due to the fact that they are made bigger than several other Oriental rugs and also are woven in light and also pastel shades.

These are just a sampling of the plethora of options you will have when you enter the world of hand-made rugs. It's my objective to get you started here, not limit your possibilities. Find your style, your preference, your particular niche - whatever establishes your curiousity ablaze.

Collecting as an Investment

Anything that is initial, unique, authentic and also is wanted by greater than one person is a financial investment. If you have a painting developed by a master artist, it's an artwork however because of its rarity and credibility, and it's also a financial investment. Johnson & Johnson equities are fairly scarce (there is a restricted supply), they produce normal earnings and also are a share in a company and also society that is one-of-a-kind, making it a financial investment. A beachfront residential property on St. Barts, a ski cottage in Vancouver or an industrial building at a busy intersection are all investments. A 1961 Austin Healey 3000 checks all the financial investment boxes. Gold. No more - or extremely couple of - of any of these points are being made as well as in time, their worth rises.

When you get a hand-made carpet from an original carpet weaving nation, you know you're going to have the ability to appreciate everything your life. Your kids are mosting likely to appreciate it. When you require to scale down in retired life, you might give the rug to a participant of your family, your youngsters, or your grandchildren and also what they have will certainly deserve a whole lot greater than what you originally paid for it. That boost in value just comes from rugs made in initial weaving nations.

This is something that I locate remarkable and also interesting. There is often a huge opportunity when you can get an authentic handmade "genuine" Asian rug for less than a new shade reproduction. It's actually feasible to get a semi-antique Persian carpet for the very same or much less than a brand new or brand-new recreation rug in whatever color combination is currently trendy. In addition to that, these new recreation rugs normally only last 15-20 years because they're made thinly without great stack. A top quality authentic rug that is 50 years old will certainly constantly be a far better investment than acquiring a recreation. It will last much longer (possibly for hundreds of years) and it will certainly raise in value, guaranteed.

Along with the long life as well as automatic increase in worth due to aging that a "real" carpet offers, it also has the potential to offer a lot more appreciation. Take into consideration - as the third globe expands, Oriental handmade carpets are ending up being a thing of the past. As the expense of living increases for the weavers of these carpets, they will need to bill so much for a carpet, nobody will have the ability to manage them. Tribal items are starting to vanish because their weavers are moving into the bigger cities. If things proceed as they have there is a really distinctive likelihood that tribal/nomadic pieces might vanish entirely.

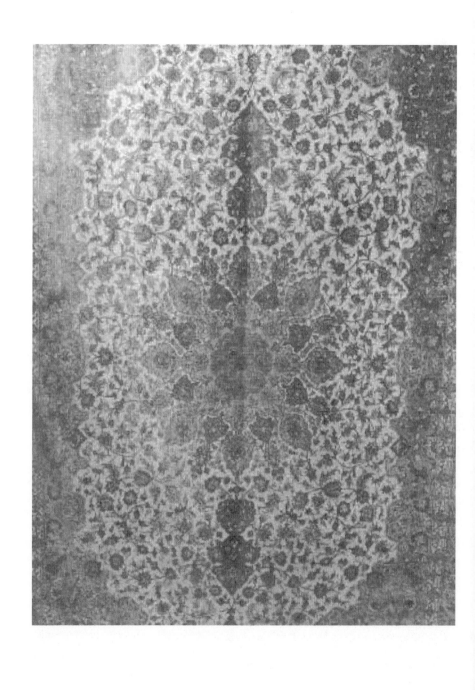

But we aren't there yet. There is still terrific possibility to acquire these initial carpets. We can still put our cash in wonderful carpets at good rates, as well as with some understanding, there are still deals to be had. We are perhaps in one of the very best durations of background to get and gather these rugs and also pass them on the next generation. If we do this with idea and treatment, we not only store our very own wide range, we also respect and also preserve the ability and also craft of these vanishing artists.

Risks of investing

The threats of purchasing rugs can be several and also complicated. However with a little education and learning as well as understanding, you can tremendously lower this danger. Likewise, understand that if you like a piece and also it is a happiness to have in your house and life, you have actually located real worth. This itself transcends money in numerous methods. Our joy as well as pleasure is really challenging to place a cost on, and I would state paying full retail for a carpet you want as well as will certainly have for generations is not risk, it's a great financial investment, despite whether it's a "bargain.".

As for overpayment risk, this market is so opaque that you can as well as likely will get taken, quite honestly, right here or abroad. In all my years of being in this organization I have actually heard customers state they intend to take a trip abroad to rack up excellent deals. I have not had but one customer in 40 years successfully take a trip abroad and work out a bargain on an extraordinary rug. This is a prevalent as well as long-lasting mistaken belief that taking a trip overseas reduces risk. More frequently, trying to acquire carpets this way increases it. You might think that traveling to a nation where handcrafted rugs are indigenously generated, as well as the weavers desire American dollars, will be to your monetary benefit. But I can state certainly you would be incorrect.

Understand that the carpet trade is essentially over a thousand years of ages and Westerners have been taking a trip to these lands in an attempt to buy stunning carpets on the economical for equally as lengthy. Keep this in mind. It's an ancient sector as old as the city wall surfaces. A crafted network. From the taxi you extract from the airport terminal or train terminal to the hotel and also to the unusual. You're not the first, not by a slim chance. This is not to impugn the track record of these dealerships, taximen, hoteliers and also tourist guide. They just know what the market will certainly bear and they recognize Westerners are lambs to the craft of negotiating. Expertise of the rug market, just how rugs are distressed or made to look antique, just how to bargain, and also the dealer markup is their purview, not your own. Their trade is not rugs - it is parting Westerners from their dollars, euros and pounds. Think of it as a great game and also do not be dissuaded or upset, it simply is. I do not claim this to dissuade you from travelling to rug creating countries. Please do and also with wonderful delight. Make memories you will certainly value for the rest of your days. Check out the marketplaces. But rather than shopping a carpet at discount, acquire something as a keepsake. A suggestion of that wonderful trip you took with the love of your life.

Currently I've been informing you that you must begin acquiring rugs to truly comprehend what you're doing as well as yet you should not most likely to carpet producing nations trying to find carpets - well then, what are you expected to do? Exactly how in the world will you have the ability to produce a collection?

This is precisely why you require a trusted merchant/dealer to collaborate with. Certainly it will look like I'm recommending this for my own advantage, but inevitably, it's for the customer's advantage. A customer of Asian rugs needs a person that can assist browse this market. When you locate a terrific dealer - one who listens to what you are searching for, assists you choose based upon your preferences, takes note of what you like, that collaborates with you as well as appreciates your budget, and who attempts to enlighten you about your acquisitions - you will be able to create a beautiful, and useful, collection.

Something I have actually observed regarding Americans is that they are taken in with getting a deal. Truthfully, Persians are the same method. We like a deal. Yet we additionally understand that it takes a lot of knowledge as well as ability acquired over years of experience in a subject to comprehend sufficient about this sort of market to get a deal by yourself. If you think of it for a minute, "acquiring retail" in the rug market is usually mosting likely to make the most sense. To start with, as an individual consumer, you are not mosting likely to have the ability to acquire in the quantity needed for wholesale rates. There is basically no other way around this. When I go on a purchasing journey, I constantly obtain at the very least 150 rugs worth between $150,000 - $200,000 from 5 or 6 different suppliers. It's extremely not likely that a person will desire or be able to do the same. And also as a private consumer, unless you have done substantial research as the majority of brokers have, 8 or more hrs a day for years, it will be incredibly tough for you to accurately value a rug. Rather than considering trying to buy " wholesale" as well as get a "bargain," I motivate my clients to see purchasing from a trustworthy broker as buying for value and also a fair cost. The solution, education and learning as well as guarantee you get utilizing an experienced broker/dealer will certainly assist you develop a handcrafted rug collection that will certainly appreciate throughout the years.

Decorating vs collecting vs investing

There are people who purchase rugs strictly for decoration, and this is completely great. Their need hinges on developing a gorgeous home as well as carpets are part of that. These people are looking mainly at colors, which in designing, modification frequently.

Concerning every five years, designers and also house owners come into our store as well as request rugs with a certain shade combination. These are not enthusiasts. A lot of them want a top quality carpet, however their primary concern is how a rug chooses the rest of their design, instead of the background, construction and also the story of the carpet.

After that there are customers that are a bit different. When they initially come to me, possibly they need carpets for a large home they simply bought or they believe they desire an asian rug to go in their living-room. At first they could be mostly worried about shade and what "goes" with what they have, however with time, as well as occasionally quickly, this modifications.

After these individuals acquire a rug, or a couple of carpets, they start to have an passion in them. They would like to know even more about the patterns, the way the rugs are made, the products and also the age of the rugs. They wonder about why one carpet that looks really fine could be cheaper than another rug that looks very crude. Or why a tiny rug would be better than a large rug. They have an interest in the shades and also icons, how the carpets are utilized and also need to know the stories behind the carpets. They invest hrs in our shop, experiencing heaps of rugs, look up at the clock and ask in a stunned tone, "where did the time go?"

These are budding collection agencies, and I have actually had the benefit to assist many along this trip as my customers. They begin to have a preferred kind or sorts of rugs from one of the genuine carpet making countries. They start visiting antique shops to see if they can locate something fascinating, something uncommon. I like when they bring these rugs back to me to ask my viewpoint; sometimes they've discovered a real surprise treasure. They begin being able to recognize rugs from various parts of the globe, and also various periods of time. They make use of carpets on their floors however additionally present carpets on their wall surfaces as design. They intend to invest all their disposable income on rugs. They begin taking trips to rug making nations to witness carpets being made.

The real turning indicate me, however, for these clients who begin to fall in love with rugs, is when they comprehend something carpet dealerships will tell every consumer, yet few will certainly pay attention - when you decorate your house, you begin with the rug you enjoy initially and "construct the space" around the carpet. The furniture, art work, home window treatments, paint, all of it is selected to match the rug. That is the minute I recognize someone has gone from having an interest to being an enthusiast. When their carpet collection comes to be the central emphasis of developing their house. Collection agencies wish to be bordered by rugs, showcase them to highlight their charm. They want to see them every morning as well as night, appreciate them, appreciate being familiar with them as well as delight in living with them via the years as the carpets increase in specialness.

There is quite a bit of overlap in individuals who "accumulate" rugs and also individuals who "purchase" rugs, for precisely this reason; if you buy a quality carpet, which is the only sort of rug an enthusiast would certainly acquire, it will value in value with appropriate care. This is ensured. The older a well made, one of a kind rug gets, the more valuable it comes to be. There is no exemption. It begins as important as well as obtains more so with age. What actually separates these two kinds of individuals is heart. The heart of an enthusiast is oriented to the elegance of the rugs, their uniqueness as well as superb attractiveness. The heart of a financier is extra drawn to these items for acquiring and also maintaining value. A financier will get exactly the exact same kinds of carpets that a collector will, because they will certainly both be trying to find lovely top quality rugs, they will certainly just experience the rugs in a different way. That said, a collection agency can absolutely be excited by the idea that his collection of "have to have," distinctive, unusual as well as lovely hand made authentic carpets value in value each year. Truly among the most exciting settings to be in is to be able to accumulate something stunning that you like, enjoy it and see it not only hold its worth, but rise in worth over time.

Starting your Collection

It's totally possible to merely head out and also start purchasing carpets, and also this is the way that several collection agencies obtain their beginning. While possible, I assume it's preferable to have some fundamental background knowledge prior to purchasing that very first rug. This will enable you to acquire with intention, which will certainly deepen your collecting experience along with offering you confidence that your very first acquisition is a high quality purchase.

Age

Age is an extremely essential point to take into consideration when collecting as well as investing in rugs. There are three age categories:

New:
A "new" carpet is not necessarily what you would certainly connect with the word "brand-new." This kind of rug could have been made yesterday or it could have been made 50 years ago. Some in business also describe a rug this age as "utilized." I like the term "new," because a high quality rug that is kept well shouldn't have damage. It's not "utilized" similarly an appliance could be "made use of" - on its means to being worn. When talking about a rug, one that is "utilized" gets on its method to coming to be more valuable.

Semi-antique:
A "semi-antique" rug is in between 50-100 years of ages. To me, this is one of the most fascinating age variety of rugs. Two different carpets can be "semi-antique," however one can be 60 years of ages, which implies it has another 40 years before it's an "antique," and another can be 90 years old as well as have only ten more years before it's an "antique." Rugs in the semi-antique variety are an incredible opportunity for today's enthusiasts. I typically encourage my clients to buy rugs that are 75-80 years old. These carpets are often less costly than antique rugs, yet the majority of my customers can expect to live long enough to see them become "antique." When you get an 80 year-old item, take great treatment of it, enjoy its appeal

in your house for two decades, and essentially over night its worth can increase, that is one of the actual thrills of gathering.

Antique:
An "antique" carpet is any carpet that mores than 100 years of ages, which naturally is a big variety of carpets. These rugs are the reward of the carpet world as well as are constantly one of the most beneficial when they are in excellent problem, in some cases also if they are worn. Obviously, the better shape they are in, the better they will certainly be, which is among the factors acquiring semi-antique can be so exciting; if you buy an even more affordable semi-antique in excellent problem and afterwards take care of it appropriately, you will certainly have a fine antique art piece.

This is an uncommon opportunity to enhance the worth of your possessions just by taking good care of them.

What is constantly sad for me is to have clients that got new rugs 25 years earlier and assume they have an antique rug. When I consider it, I need to inform them, no this is not, this is still a new rug and also has a long way to go. When you purchase an all new rug, you're not visiting it to be a hundred years old. Rugs outlive us numerous times over. The earliest rug in existence is 1200 years old.

What gives a carpet value?

This is a tricky concern. We have actually checked out the various classifications for age, and also age is where a lot of a rug's worth comes from. Specifically, when a carpet goes from a carpet "semi-antique" to "antique" the worth can increase fairly a great deal. The age of a rug matters a great deal in providing it worth.

But it would be erroneous to believe that age is the only thing that makes a carpet important. Lots of believe that the number of knots per square inch in a carpet, or the excellence of the weave, is what provides it worth. I have actually listened to some collection agencies proclaim the even more knots per square inch, automatically the more valuable the rug. While a finely knotted rug is absolutely a point of terrific charm, it is not the only point that offers a carpet its value.

The next thing we could check out is the materials made use of to make the carpet, as well as the handiwork. There are various kinds of woollen and silk that offer a carpet value. There is a kind of wool that originates from the first shearing of a baby lamb's neck, called Kork woollen. This woollen is very fine as well as expensive and also a carpet made from this woollen will have a specific quantity of value simply because an unskilled or unartful rug maker will not use such a pricey product. Another fine material is silk. Silk rugs are attractive and typically thought to be better than woollen, yet also this is not necessarily real.

The ability of the rugmaker will affect a carpet's worth, and a great weave in a rug with a well-executed, intricate pattern will present a certain amount of worth. The size will also contribute in the worth, yet of course that depends as well because a little rug that is 200 years old as well as constructed from the finest woollen will certainly deserve greater than a big carpet that was made in the last two decades.

Truthfully, it is inevitably the rarity, the individuality of the carpet, that offers it value. Materials, workmanship, design are all important. Yet absolutely nothing compares to rarity when it comes to valuing carpets. There are more youthful antique rugs that will certainly have worth due to their materials and building and construction, once we reach a specific age array, these things come to be less important. At the end of the day, the age of a rug is most likely to be one of the most causal element, naturally, since the older a carpet is, the more probable it is to be rare. Allow me provide you an example of exactly how this adjustments with time.

Serapis are one of the most beneficial rugs today. The even more contemporary models of these rugs are called Hariz, from the Hariz component of Iran. A Serapi is actually simply an older generation of Hariz, there is no "Serapi" area of Iran. Around 200 years back when rugs were being delivered from Iran to the US, they would be covered in a Hariz Serapi to safeguard them. These Serapis went to one-time made use of like the brown paper used to wrap an useful art item, as well as ruled out useful. Now, they are so rare that they are amongst the most expensive rugs to be located. They are not carefully made, the majority of having only 50- 60 knots per square inch with a brief heap. And also yet, they are best enthusiast pieces. A large Serapi can bring $20,000 - $30,000 retail relying on its problem. This is a terrific example of how the value of a rug is totally subjective and also how much irregularity is involved in determining its well worth.

Handmade Rug Construction

Rugs can take years to make. Woven by hand, knot by knot, the craft is old and has been passed down through generations of craftsmens for actually millenia. While the patterns of these art work can be very detailed as well as difficult, the procedure is reasonably simple. Let's take a look.

How rugs are made

Frequently, when a weaver starts to make a carpet, the carpet has actually been appointed by an exporter or dealer. A down payment will be made on the carpet, a dimension figured out, along with a pattern. Patterns differ widely, depending on whether they are city made, village or tribal and the country they originate from.

Some styles are intricate, requiring a drawn pattern (generally on chart paper). The ones that include a facility medallion with two halves that mirror each various other, are actually used just a quarter of the pattern itself; the one quarter will be turned right into the four various quadrants of the carpet and oriented so the weaver can follow it to develop the complete carpet. These designs are commonly developed by people who concentrate on pattern making, having well-honed skills in crafting the character of carpets.

When a pattern is attracted using chart paper, each square of the paper is colored and also corresponds to one knot of the carpet. The weaver uses these tinted squares to establish the pattern of the rug as well as follows it to create the end product.

Some carpets are so merely designed that they do not require an attracted pattern. These are generally tiny tribal carpets and will be geometric, as opposed to curvilinear. They usually consist of usual pictures from tribal life, like a dance lady or a pet dog or possibly a lamb.

After determining the pattern of the carpet to be made, the weaver will

obtain the materials to produce the rug; wool, silk, cotton, occasionally also animal hair. Shade is exceptionally crucial in Oriental carpets, and lots of weavers dye their very own yarn. In cities, it's more common for weavers to buy pre-dyed products, with nomadic tribal people, the weavers usually color their very own yarns.

Carpets are basically three parts: the warp, the knots, and the weft. The warp is the carpet structure as well as can be constructed from wool, wool and also silk, silk, or cotton. Many clients want to know if one product makes a carpet more valuable - for example, is a carpet constructed out of silk better than a carpet made out of wool? The answer is constantly, "it depends." Silk is an extremely fine product, yet a brand-new silk carpet is not always better than an older wool carpet of rare design. Worth is always situational.

When a size and also pattern are identified, the weaving impend is set with what is called the warp. This is a series of rows of stuck product, constructed of cotton, woollen or often silk. The product is wrapped onto the impend and also completion of the warp will ultimately make the edge on each end of the rug when it's completed. This is the start of the structure of the rug.

When the warp is set on the loom, the weaver produces completion of the carpet, which is called kilim. Exactly how it's made varies depending on where the rugs are from. Some weavers use fringe only on one end. Some have edge on both ends. Some areas create carpets that have a small kilim end and afterwards the various other end will certainly have fringe. As you start to recognize various carpet ends as well as various kilim and fringe styles, it will assist you recognize the origins of a rug.

With the warp on the impend as well as the kilim in place, the weaver can currently begin to celebrate a marriage of the carpet, of which there will certainly be thousands in an individual piece, all done by hand. Every one of the little squares on a pattern is colored to signify the shade of the knot that needs to be placed in the carpet. As the weaver begins, whatever row is being worked with - for example, 3 red knots, 3 white, one blue, duplicated throughout - when the row is finished, the pattern is established.

When a row of knots is finished, the weaver will add what is known as the weft, a thread that runs in between the warp threads, horizontally on top of the knots.

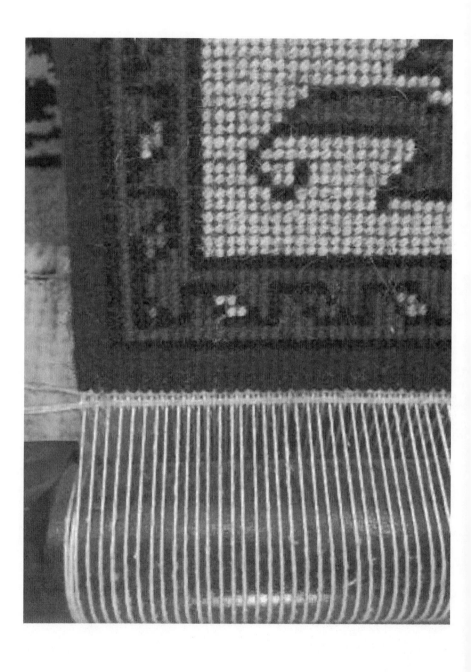

The weft inevitably holds the rug with each other and also offers the carpet its thickness. It's likewise where a great deal of variation in rugs happens, since the weft tension can differ dramatically, weaver to weaver. This distinction is particularly noticeable when checking out the rear of the rug.

While the warp is what the knots are tied on, the weft is what packs the knots right into the rug and holds them in place. In some weaving areas like Bidjar in Iran, the weavers will certainly take a hammer and pack the weft down so securely, producing such a strong, dense and sturdy carpet, that it can be put in the busiest entranceway of the globe's most preferred resort as well as still look brand new after 100 years.

As a row is finished, the weaver will accompany and also clip the added product off after putting in the weft as well as loading it down. This is finished with an unique set of scissors made for this purpose. Then begins the next row, and also this continues until the rug is completed.

Functioning from one side to the other, knots are incorporated succession till the pattern is completed.

Occasionally, a weaver will authorize and also date a carpet, typically at the top of the rug when it's done. As previously mentioned, rugs can take a year or even more to complete.

Although it might have taken two years to end up a rug, however the date on it will certainly be the day it's completed. Actually, all-time low of a carpet might be two years (or even more) older than the top of the same carpet.

Many people believe a rug with a trademark is worth more than a rug without one. A trademark doesn't alter the real value yet, it can be a nice point to have, much more as an uniqueness. Some dealers will try to inform their clients that a rug is a whole lot more valuable than because of the trademark, yet in truth it is not.

One exemption to this are rugs that are considered work of arts. These rugs will typically have the name of the beginning city and the name of the weaver on it. This is even more typical in city rugs. As an example, a pure silk Guhm will have the word "Guhm" woven as well as the name of the weaver. Turkish silk Hereke carpets will often have "Hereke" on them. While this remains in component due to the fact that weavers have satisfaction in their job, it is mostly customized extra than anything else.

There is an additional false impression concerning hand-crafted rugs, especially I have actually located, in the United States. People typically believe, as a result of the little knots in a great carpet, that small children are making the rugs. They think that little fingers are called for to make such little knots. This is absolutely not true. Something as sophisticated as well as fine as a carpet with hundreds or sometimes hundreds of knots per square inch can never ever be made by a young child. A weaver should make rugs a whole life time to be able to weave something so precise and also great. It's difficult to recognize the number of rugs these weavers have made, the ones that are making these small knots, probably hundreds. In my career, I have actually seen carpets that have 2,500 knots per square inch. It is absolutely mind-boggling. Feel confident, though, only a weaver with remarkable experience, a real experienced master, might knot such a carpet.

On the various other hand, many individuals assume since a carpet is loosely woven it is not an excellent rug. This likewise isn't true. Vintage Serapi Hariz were discussed prior to; these rugs may have somewhere between 50 and also 60 knots per square inch, which is an extremely loosened weave, but they are amongst the most valuable items that exist today. Serapis are so valuable that they are one of the few rugs that can be worth restoring. A lot of rugs when they are harmed, are just worth salvaging, safeguarding them from more damages. Serapis can really enhance in value, despite the expense of the repair.

There are 2 different sort of knots.There is a Turkish knot and also there is a Persian knot.The rugs made in Turkey, Kurdistan, Azerbaijan and also components of Iran use this type of knot, which is consistent, balanced and extremely solid. The heap in rugs woven with this type of knot has a tendency to be quite thick and also also. A Persian knot is extremely different and also provides itself to producing finer rugs, with greater knots per square inch and also elaborate patterns. Half of the knot is connected about the warp as well as half is loose, providing the knot asymmetry and less mass, which can then be pushed together really securely with the weft, producing that higher density of knots per square inch.

There are 3 sort of carpet without knots, the very first 2 being called "kilim" and "aubusson." These are level weave designs of rug, as well as it's the weft of the rug, instead of rows of knots, that composes the pattern. These type of rugs are made in a number of the same locations where you will find authentic knotted carpets - Russia, Turkey, Iran. The colors in the carpet will certainly usually inform the tale of where the carpets have actually been made. The third no-knot rug kind is called "soumak," and it's rather intriguing due to the fact that it is nearly an in between kind of rug. It does not use a pile like a knotted carpet, but it isn't as level as a kilim or aubusson. The rug is made by weaving the wool thread around two warp strands, backward and forward, as well as packing it down, and there is no knot. This kind of weaving develops a fragile rug because if one part of the carpet ends up being broken or weak, the entire carpet might unwind as there are no knots holding the rug with each other.

While several rugs are clipped by the weaver throughout the weaving process, with some rugs extra yarns and threads are not clipped and rather, a shearer will certainly be employed to sculpt the heap and also reveal the pattern. This is a very competent setting; one mistake as well as a rug that has actually taken a year or more to weave can be messed up by being sheared as well reduced. It takes years to establish this accurate and exacting ability. When a rug has been sheared, or otherwise if it's been clipped by the weaver, it obtains "cleaned," which is a defeating out of accumulated dirt from the air and clipped or sheared yarns, as well as it prepares to go to the dealer.

How rugs come to market

The Oriental rug market absolutely relies on the dealers as well as broker/dealers. As covered above, a rug can take a year or even more to make, depending upon its size and the fineness of the weave. While the weaver is essential to creating carpets, it's the wholesaler who actually finances the production of carpets

In Iran, as an example, a wholesaler will most likely to a weaver, giving a pattern and also pay a deposit for the weaver to start job. Once the carpet is about one 3rd finished, the dealer will certainly pay an additional installment for the carpet. After that when a bit more of the carpet is done, the weaver will certainly obtain an additional repayment from the dealer. With a system of breakthroughs, dealers remain to buy more of a carpet up until it is ended up. On a check out to Iran after moving to the US, I met my great-uncle's granddaughter, a girl in her twenties. Walking into her home I saw 2 looms with carpets concerning halfway completed. She told me that she was weaving them which she had currently been paid over half of what she was offering them for, despite the fact that the rugs.

were only half ended up, and also this was the typical layaway plan for all the carpets she made. Wholesalers are important to the weaving process, making sure that carpets can be generated as well as weavers can remain to make rugs. It's a really synergistic partnership which needs enormous trust fund between the two events. Weavers need dealers to fund production, and also dealers require weavers to produce product.

As soon as a dealer has the rugs, they can be delivered overseas - to the US for example - to another wholesaler who can after that sell them to shop dealers. In the 40 years of being in business I've constructed partnerships with numerous dealers, mostly in the eastern US. Some broker/dealers will make buying trips overseas to buy carpets for resale, and also initially of my career, I did also. At some point, though, I found that buying rugs from a trustworthy wholesaler in the United States gives me the very best high quality and worth that I can hand down to my clients.

At once I would certainly go to New york city a number of times a year to do organization with dealers, the majority of whom have actually currently progressed right into partners and also pals. As soon as a strong partnership is developed in between a wholesaler and a dealership, the dealer will allow the supplier to return any stock that isn't marketing in the store. The first day of my acquiring trips was constantly to do these returns.

At 9 a.m. the next day, I 'd come back to start purchasing brand-new rugs. I would invest three days taking a look at rugs at the various wholesalers I collaborate with there, throughout the day, for hours, going through the rugs and stating "yes" or "no" to every of them. The "yes" carpets would be put aside for me for the first 2 days. After I finished buying in those two days, the last day would certainly be utilized to return through the rugs I 'd chosen and pick the most effective of those carpets. After the last option was made, I would certainly prepare to "make the run" back home.

Making sure the wholesalers understood that I would certainly be coming back early the next early morning to take the inventory, I 'd fill up the associate gas. Early in the early morning, I 'd choose every little thing up and after that I would certainly secure the truck as well as clear out of Manhattan, not picking up a very long time. Commonly I would certainly not quit my truck for over 300 miles.

There is a good reason for this seemingly odd behavior, and also it's not due to the fact that I simply intended to get a jump on website traffic; it was fairly usual for thieves to see a vehicle being loaded up with rugs as well as follow the truck with the purpose of hijacking it.These burglars are smart, they understand the worth of this cargo. This has actually never happened to me, yet I know people who pulled in to obtain gas with a truckful of carpets and also, coming out after paying for their gas, the truck would be gone. I would certainly constantly see to it I had adequate gas to go 300- 400 miles without stopping. My approach was to make them give up or perhaps possibly run out of gas themselves. This most likely seems outrageous to the ordinary person, but I promise you, this takes place. Selling Asian carpets can be a crazy service.

I share stories similar to this with you since they are amusing, but there is a lot more relevance to it. It's another reason that, as you are making your collection, to undergo a reputable dealership. Individuals who have actually been in the business for many years, understand these risks as well as exactly how to prevent them, they add worth. The temptation to "remove the intermediary" in any type of large purchase is strong, and I recognize. However in the world of Oriental rugs, the "middleman" - the dealer as well as his or her knowledge and knowledge - can be your best friend.

Dye And Design

Shade as well as stylistic elements are as vital in a hand-crafted rug as the building of it. If a rug is made from unbalanced product or inadequately bound, it will not be a beautiful carpet. At the exact same time, if a carpet is perfectly built with every knot in its specific location, but the coloring is off, it will certainly also fall short to be an attractive rug.

Dyes

Fundamentally there are two type of dyes for handmade rugs, "vegetable" as well as "chemical." Vegetable dyes are made from plants and animals. Greater than being definitively "veggie," they are more properly described as "non-chemical." At one time, vegetable dye was the only choice offered. These kinds of dyes are very variable and require a simple yet exact and also practically user-friendly process, through which the thread is plunged into boiling veggie color and is delegated simmer for a specific amount of time.

As the thread is steamed, it takes on coloring that is essentially intense, based on the amount of time invested in the steaming color as well as additionally the particular traits of just how the particular set of dye was made. One origin or animal can be a little a lot more extreme or a little bit more muted than one more of the very same dimension, and as little as a minute of added boiling can cause variations in color. The people who concentrate on this craft recognize the dishes as well as times. Like a chef recognizes just how to prepare food for fragile and refined flavors, somebody that dyes woollen will certainly understand exactly how to cook it for delicate as well as refined variations in shade.

Veggie passing away is a real art kind that is ending up being much less and also less common as we relocate right into the future. Now, it is still feasible to acquire rugs woven with materials colored with veggie dyes. In the future, it's nearly unpreventable that rugs made with vegetable dyed products will certainly enhance in worth, solely since the ability of veggie dying will certainly end up being less and also less widespread as less as well as fewer artisans tint their materials in this manner.

One hundred thirty years earlier, chemical dyes began being made. These dyes are made exclusively from chemicals, as well as are much more commonly referred to as "chromide." The most considerable difference in between the two types of dye is color uniformity in the ended up thread, both at first when the carpet is woven new, and afterwards likewise with time as the rug ages. Chemical dye is very constant. A specialist wool or silk dye craftsmen can make amazing colors, exactly the very same over and over again, using a chemical dye created with an accurate formula. This accuracy makes a carpet attire and very fine in its beauty.

Maybe one of the most substantial point that differentiates veggie color and also chemical color is just how they discolor over time. A vegetable color will certainly start with more variant and also will constantly have much more variation as it ages, which can be attractive as well as exciting to see. It's like a window into a previous world. Well dyed chemical products will discolor evenly, which is not fundamentally better or worse than what happens with veggie color, merely different.

There are some who will suggest that rugs made with veggie dyed materials are better. This is rubbish. There are stunning and also valuable pieces that are woven with chemically colored products, and also as a matter of fact, an almost unlimited variant of colors can be developed with colorful dyes. There is a prejudice versus them, which is unfounded and unfavorable. The only factor in this day and also age that an item made with veggie dyed material is since veggie dye is what is readily available, not since the vegetable dye procedure transcends. Similar to the knotting and also construction of the carpets, if it is finished with ability, a colorful color can be equally as lovely as well as valuable as a veggie dye.

A knowledgeable passing away procedure is very vital. If the passing away process is refrained from doing properly, whether it be from inappropriate food preparation, taking care of or rinsing, can lead to color run, which will seriously weaken the value of any kind of carpet. It additionally creates a problem from an easy functional and also practical viewpoint, because if you buy a carpet and also the colors hemorrhage or fade, the carpet is no more the carpet you acquired as well as your enjoyment of it will certainly be decreased.

As soon as the preferred shades are achieved, the wool appears of the color and is dried. The last step in this procedure is cleaning the wool, which is very vital. Cleaning the woollen obtains the dye deposit out of the dye as well as assists maintain the shades from pursuing the rug is woven.

One way to test the color fastness of a rug is to wet an item of white fabric (a bandana will certainly function, or any kind of piece of white fabric) and also massage it over each of the colors in a carpet. If significant color comes off on the white cloth, you could have a problem. If the carpet is made from woollen tinted with vegetable color, you will obtain a little bit of shade, and also this is fine. Nevertheless, if a lot of color comes off on the cloth, the dye hasn't been well established and also you'll have trouble down the road. In many cases, you will certainly want to avoid a rug that has this capacity for shade bleed.

There is a significant exemption to this basic regulation about shade run. If you are thinking about a tribal carpet, you may still desire it for your collection. In some cases nomadic individuals, despite the fact that they are extremely competent craftsmens, for whatever reason will not have actually had the ability to rinse the woollens enough to prevent color run. If this is the case, you must have the ability to take the carpet to a professional cleaner to take the excess color out of the rug without doing any kind of damage to it.

One of the distinct high qualities of the veggie dye is the sensation referred to as "abrash." This is the variation in color triggered by the different color "great deals" of vegetable color stated before. Veggie dyes will begin as various shades of shade from the minute they are produced and afterwards with time, they will certainly discolor at different rates, based on for how long they were cooked when they were colored. The abrash of a carpet is just one of the ways you can inform you have a "real" rug that has actually been hand-made. Abrash occurs flat throughout a rug as dye great deals modification. When abrash occurs in the incorrect instructions of a carpet, it's highly likely that the abrash has actually been done purposefully to make the carpet look older than it is.

Design

There are a number of various fundamental layouts for an Oriental rug. While the facility medallion mirrored carpet is very common, there are various other kinds of layouts that are rather beautiful. Usually these carpets, with a couple of exemptions, will certainly have either two or three borders around the entire boundary of the carpet, with an area in the center.

Different areas certainly have particular layouts, but among one of the most interesting aspects of Oriental rugs is that the craft and tradition is very old, and also it is a cottage market. While specific towns as well as tribes would have "their own" designs, as people wed and also relocated, they brought these styles with them. Weavers grow up finding out the craft and so their "hometown" components currently end up being included right into their brand-new family members's styles.

Below are a few of the different style types you will certainly locate as you get rugs for your collection. They are as varied as the areas they originate from.

Around Layout:.
As the name suggests, these carpets have a design throughout the area of the rug, and also can have many boundaries of a reflective design around the area.

The repeating components differ depending upon where the rug is made. The popular "elephant impact" is round as well as medallion-like, while the paisley form is drop. Both of these components are extensively found in the around layout.

Center Medallion:

Already stated, this carpet includes a medallion in the center of the carpet's area as well as each of the four quadrants is a mirror image and normally features numerous borders around the area.

Repeat Medallion:.
The repeat medallion additionally has a medallion as its centerpiece, yet

rather of a single medallion around which the rest of the pattern is constructed, the field will consist of three and sometimes extra medallions straight. These patterns can still be mirrors of each other and also will certainly also have some sort of boundary.

Around Medallion/Design:.
This rug layout contains a field of smaller sized medallions throughout the area. While the pattern is still in proportion, it has less of a mirror image look than the central as well as repeat medallion carpets. These carpets will sometimes feature more than one medallion design duplicating in tandem with one more throughout the field.

Vase Design:
This is an old layout, very carefully woven and rare. A lot of the vase design antique rugs were appointed for royalty. The layout can include a flower holder and also usually does, however it additionally features intricate floral aspects as well as dynamic shade. The flower holder element might be prominent, extremely subtle or perhaps simply hinted at and still be thought about a vase style.

Tree of Life:.
The tree of life style is reasonably unusual, and also can include a medallion in the middle of the area with mirrored halves of the rug, there will simply be a curvilinear tree style included on both halves of the carpet too.

Pictorial Layout:.
A photographic rug functions real people and things rather than patterns and shapes. While a number of the rugs we've considered above have floral or organic concepts that technically feature "things," their depiction has a tendency towards the abstract. A photographic design element will be well specified as well as well-known - for instance, a boat looks like a boat as one could paint or draw it, not an abstract depiction of a watercraft. People look like people, several of them will certainly also stand for well-known or widely known people of the day, or aristocracy.

Prayer rugs

Carpets can be greater than simply comfort, decor as well as a shop of riches. They can additionally be devices of our spiritual life. The prayer carpet is a prime example of just how something that many people consider just ornamental or utilitarian can be utilized in a really various method.

Muslims, who practice the faith of Islam, most frequently utilize what are called petition carpets. In Islam, the faithful are contacted us to prayer 5 times daily, and these prayers are taken really seriously. To come close to God, Islam shows that the muslim requirements to execute a routine cleansing and also the prayer rug can work as a way to accentuate this sanitation, keeping the prayerful from touching the floor or ground.

How are prayer rugs different from other oriental rugs

Many individuals have a false impression of what a petition rug is, believing it to be a really small carpet, possibly 2 feet by three feet. Actually, even for somebody that is just five foot 3 inches, a 2 foot by three foot carpet is not large sufficient to hope on. The worshiper needs enough length to be able to stoop right down to the flooring as well as be able to put their temple down on the front of the rug. For even the most petite adult, the minimal size required is about three feet by 5 feet.

Unlike the majority of various other Asian carpets, the petition carpet is directional. Some Chinese and French rugs are directional, however the majority of Oriental rugs consist of top and lower halves that are like mirrors. The prayer carpet design is "sharp," as well as unlike the majority of carpets, it can be oriented to be appropriate side up or upside-down, the layout going one method, getting more slim on top.

The pattern can be very primitive or it can be much more in-depth as well as finely performed, but it will certainly always become extra slim going upwards. The top of the carpet commonly has areas marked in the weaving pattern to place the hands when praying, on either side of the spot noted for the head.

When one goes to pray, the rug is oriented to make sure that the head is pointed towards Mecca. In a mosque, the instructions is suggested by what's called the " mihrab," which is a niche created in the wall surface that straight encounters Mecca. Some prayer rugs will certainly depict a mihrab in their style, further mirroring the objective of the rug.

Once oriented towards Capital, the worshiper will certainly after that stoop on the back component of the carpet and bow down to pray, positioning the hands on the pens of the carpet and the directly its pen. The rug acts both as a floor covering for praying, along with a guide for exactly how to put the body during petition.

Prayer carpet designs themselves are vast and differed. There are official rugs, very finely detailed, and also casual carpets, with even more primitive patterns. Some rugs are geometric with markers for body positioning that are essentially simply squares or rectangular shapes. Others consist of an intricate tree of life layout, with far more elaborate pens for body positioning. There are also some prayer carpets that have a mosque as the area marker for the head.

While there is no one country that makes remarkable prayer carpets, Turkey is especially known for its petition carpets. Also still, there are muslims throughout the world as well as all the major handmade carpet generating areas create stunning petition carpets.

Just how are they utilized.

Sincere Muslims pray five times a day. This method is called the pillar of salat (Islam is based upon 5 pillars of obedience to God) as well as the prayer rug is an important part of the practice. The first prayer of the day is called Salat al-fajr and takes place pre-dawn, right before sunup. The 2nd petition, Salat al-zuhr, is right at mid-day when the sun is at its peak. The 3rd petition, Salat al-' asr, takes place in the mid-day. Salat al-maghrib, the 4th petition of the day, is just after sundown. As well as the final 5th daily prayer, Salat al-' isha is between sundown and also twelve o'clock at night. One of the unifying collective high qualities of this strenuous petition timetable is that muslims are praying together, even when not in the exact same place. If someone must take a trip for work, he recognizes that his family is hoping "with" him because they are all praying at the very same time. As well as actually, all muslims when they hope at the prescribed times throughout the day, are praying with all other hoping muslims.

These carpets are very portable and a prayerful individual will certainly always take a trip.

with a prayer rug, utilizing it to pray in their resort area or momentary living quarters. Right here is an interesting fact concerning Islamic petition; if you are not welcomed or welcome in a room, you are not to hope there. If you remain in a hotel, for example, because you are paying for the space, it's "your own," so you might pray in it. However if in an undesirable setting, or a location where one does not belong - if you have actually burglarized a home, for instance - a Muslim should not pray.

While the majority of prayer carpets are longer than they are broad and created for one person, there are some interesting prayer rugs called "Saph" that are developed wider than they are long. For example, a carpet could be five feet long on the pointed size and after that fifteen or even more feet wide. The layout on these is rather different. It will certainly have a repeating pattern concerning 3 to five feet apart. This is a household prayer carpet. They are produced for families to hope together at the very same time, with the same rug, each family member belonging on the rug. Usually the other half will get on one end, the kids in the middle and also the partner on the various other end. They are not really typical but you might find one and they are well worth accumulating.

Finding Quality Rugs

When you decide to purchase your initial handmade rug, you will certainly ask "where should I locate a well made rug of high quality?" There are a few various excellent alternatives, and there are some things to be avoided.

Reputable rug merchant/dealer

My really initial suggestion for where to find quality rugs, particularly for a brand-new collection agency, is with a reliable carpet dealer. This can be an obstacle to locate. I've constantly stated there are 3 individuals you should never ever rely on - insurance coverage agents, used cars and truck salespersons, as well as carpet dealers. Certainly I'm mostly kidding as well as directly love my insurance coverage agent and also my vehicle man, but there is a reason all 3 of these careers have a poor online reputation.

Have you ever before saw just how Asian rug stores constantly seem to be going out of business? Always having 80% off sales? Whatever must go? This is why our career is often seen in such a poor light. Absolutely nothing about these "sales" holds true. The firm is not really going out of business, and while the price could be marked down 80%, it's only due to the fact that the initial (wholesale) price is market up 3000%. That's not a typo. It's really simple to make a hefty earnings when you do this kind of math.

In our shop, we will certainly supply "discount rates," however never greater than about 15 or 20%. And we never, ever before, do stress sales. What I constantly tell a new customer/client is that they need to rest on an acquisition. They must most likely to other shops and see what various other sort of prices is around, touch other rugs and also feel for top quality. Lot of times you can just really feel exactly how well a rug is made.

An additional point we do is enable our clients to take rugs residence with them, to see how they search in a space. This is typical technique for trusted dealerships (some, like myself, don't also take down payments on the rugs. This organization is built on trust fund.). If you go into a shop, ask to take a rug house and if the dealer balks or states that their rates is "today just," leave. This isn't somebody you want to work with.

I have actually been doing this for a long time, and I understand carpets truly well. I also have a stringent code; if I wouldn't have a rug and also put it in my very own house, I won't sell it in my shop. I don't desire my customers to have rugs that I would not be happy to possess. I've always stuck to this technique, and also when I'm shopping at a wholesaler, I consider myself as using my experience in behalf of my clients. I'm not simply buying points I recognize will offer, I'm purchasing something I would certainly be honored to have and have in my residence. I just buy real handmade carpets that will certainly offer enhancing worth for my clients if the carpets are well taken care of.

Once you do discover a great dealer, make good friends. Treat them well and you will certainly always be dealt with in kind. Really good carpet dealers absolutely like what we do, enjoy rugs and love other individuals that love rugs. You will discover that you have an excellent brand-new relationship.

Auctions

I got my begin at auctions. Usually, there are a few auction houses in any kind of huge city or community and also in the large ones, you'll discover several. When you understand carpets, an auction is an enjoyable area to go head-to-head with another collection agency or suppliers. Sometimes it's an antiquarian, sometimes it's an additional rug supplier, however the time-sensitive, pressure cooker of an auction scenario is where you can actually examine your carpet understanding.

When I most likely to public auctions, I'm not searching for brand-new carpets, I always search for vintages. Due to my history making carpets, I know quality building and construction and now due to 40 years in the carpet selling business, I recognize how to value rugs as well. At public auction, I need to get below wholesale in order to make a carpet worth acquiring, but a collector isn't in the same scenario. A collection agency can purchase wholesale and even a bit above when the buy is right.

Persistence is a virtue at an auction, as well as I have actually needed to educate myself to wait up until something really interesting turns up. It's an actual obstacle, and often it pays off in inconceivable means. I mosted likely to an auction in the mid- 80s which had a section consisting of boxes of things that would certainly be cost five or six bucks. I strolled into the public auction area and I saw the edge of a rug in one of the boxes. I drew it up and also quickly, my heart started battering. I might hear the blood flowing in my ears. I believed to myself, "why did they put this in here?" I put the lid back on, attempting not to give the cold shoulder and casual.

I was determined to win this auction. There was an antique dealer bidding versus me and also the video game got on. I had no suggestion if he understood what was in the box and also I attempted not to allow my nerves and also exhilaration program. We began at $5. After that $15. Lastly we concerned $100. I went to $105 and the antique dealer caved. Right then as well as there I recognized he had no idea what was actually in the box.

I paid the $105 and right after I finished paying, the dealer approached me. "I allow you have something excellent, didn't I?" as well as I claimed "oh yes - allow me reveal you something!" I folded up the corner of the rug back, relocate in a surge activity, triggering the weave of the rug to undulate it in the light.
" You see this intense yellow flash? That's gold!""

He couldn't believe it. The carpet, in a little bargain box at an auction, had component of its foundation built entirely from gold. It's probably 250 years old, a Hereke constructed from silk. I have actually had dealerships offer me upwards of $15,000 for it, yet it's except sale. It's an once-in-a-lifetime locate. It becomes part of the Ramazani household currently.

You can have a blast - and locate some actually wonderful points - at auctions.

Vintage shops

One really interesting area for collectors to try to find Oriental rugs is antique shops. By "antique stores," I indicate your standard antique shops, as well as additionally antique shopping centers, flea markets as well as retro furniture dealers.

Right here's the factor these locations can be so great for an enthusiast with interest and also perseverance. People that sell "antiques" as opposed to dealing specifically in rugs or coins or publications are generalists as well as do not always recognize the specifics of a product they might have in their inventory. So, for instance, an antique dealer could have some carpets, and also recognize normally that they are valuable because they understand the worth of antiques, yet if you recognize a little more than they do, you could be able to obtain a good deal.

One-time when I had my first store, we were slow someday and also I informed the woman that was aiding me that day that I wanted to stretch my legs and also check out the two antique shops down the street. "Are you taking your checkbook?" she teased me. She recognized me pretty well.

I walked right into my favored neighborhood shop just a couple doors down and greeted to the owner that I 'd known for a very long time. I remained in the store for concerning 3 minutes when I found a carpet on the flooring. It was practically the like the moment I saw the rug with the gold weft. I understood right away what it was. I could not discover the cost so I asked "how much for this piece?" The proprietor informed me the full rate, "but also for you, 20% less naturally!" I took out my checkbook, paid as well as in less than 5 mins, was back at my very own store with the new rug. "You're back already?"

I presented the rug and also she wheezed. It was attractive. An extremely unusual Char Mahal Bakhtiari that I purchased for less than half what I would have had the ability to market it for. A definitely stunning example of its style.

There are some people who will ask "isn't that capitalizing on somebody to buy something at much less than its real value?" I can guarantee you something, absolutely and also totally - a store owner will not market something at a cost that he does not such as. The antiquarian, who I take into consideration a pal and have massive respect for as a colleague, got that piece at a rate that allowed him to offer it to me for the price I paid. Just because I can market it in the Oriental rug market for extra, doesn't indicate he was benefited from. This is something that is very vital to remember when we are buying anything. We are never ever trying to pull a rapid one over on anyone. We are shopping at a price that makes us happy. If a person intends to sell to us at that price, we think that the same cost makes the seller delighted, or else he would certainly not agree to it.

Another terrific instance of this kind of purchasing originates from among my client/collector trainees, a boy who has a fantastic eye and a keen hunger for learning about carpets. He did a little research study on bags, which is an interesting particular niche as well as someday, while he and also his spouse remained in a little shop in a town they were visiting, he encountered a beautiful little woven Baluch bag. He handled to bargain with the shop proprietor a little, getting the price down by about 40%. The sale was made, with the shop proprietor laughing and asking the pair to make sure as well as come back the next time they remained in town. When they brought the bag to me, I knew my "pupil" had been listening; the bag was easily worth twice what he had spent for it.

This is just one of the really enjoyable components of gathering and it's a great example of how a little bit of understanding goes a lengthy means. This customer had actually been researching rugs in bits and items in his spare time for concerning a year, however he had a genuine interest and he could recognize top quality weaving when he saw it. With a bit of understanding and also a lot of perseverance, anyone can locate these little gems and have a blast doing it.

Online

Can you acquire rugs online? The short answer is "yes you can," however in reality, it's much more complex. There are 3 substantial issues with getting a rug online. One is that you probably will not have a relationship with the dealership, which places you at a distinct downside. Another is that you

can't try the rug out in your home, and also this is virtually more vital than the partnership, although these 2 things go together. Finally, images just do not properly interact the shades and also texture of the rug. I've never gotten a rug online that looked like the photo. I do not understand precisely why it's difficult to develop online photos that are a true depiction of these rugs, yet, in my experience, the photos are never right.

If you understand a dealer in a far-off place, and you trust them, you might be able to efficiently purchase a carpet from them. You will be able to inform the supplier what it is you are searching for, they will recognize your tastes as well as perhaps also your house, permitting them to let you know whether a rug will be a good fit for you. At the same time, if you discover an online supplier that will allow you return the carpet free of charge, after that you can check the carpet in your room the same way you would take a rug residence and attempt it in your regional market.

Both of these circumstances are not likely, though, as well as actually it's not an excellent choice to get a carpet online. You could feel like you have actually discovered a terrific rug at a really affordable price, however the chances of your getting a substandard or improperly valued rug are high. As tempting as it may be to purchase rugs online, I suggest that you shop with a local supplier you can trust. It may seem like you are paying more, yet I assure that in the end you will really conserve money by mosting likely to a reliable local dealership who can lead you to a carpet you like. The most effective dealers are instructors in mind, and they will intend to impart their understanding to you - make certain to take advantage of the opportunity, not just to purchase the excellent carpet, but to learn the stories behind it.

Overseas

Component of the charm of these classic art items is that they can take you to away lands to see individuals and places not even desired for. It's just all-natural that we want to drop in where these rugs are made and also satisfy the people closest to their creation. Not surprisingly, it would certainly motivate everybody to travel to the significant and also not so significant rug making cities as well as villages. It's absolutely fantastic and you'll always remember the experience, something that's priceless. That being stated, please drop in the countries, take lots of pictures, make your memories, however leave the carpets at the fetes. Let me share among numerous tales regarding trying to "purchase wholesale" by purchasing carpets in the neighborhood overseas markets.

This was in the late 1980's. I had actually just unlocked my door to open my look for the day. Initial thing in the early morning, right when I opened up, a woman involved the shop. She told me she had 2 rugs she desired me to appraise.

I walked with her to her vehicle, obtained the carpets as well as told her if she had some tasks to run, it will certainly take about an hour to assess the carpets. She left and I brought them in, opened them up as well as appraised them. I had them prepared when she came back in. Of course she paid me for my service and after that she looked at the assessment. I told her both of the rugs together evaluated for $12,500.

A black cloud came by her face. She stated "I informed him not to do it!" I stated, "you informed that not to do it?" She claimed, I informed my spouse not to do it. I was curious, so I asked what she meant.

" Late last evening, we just came back from Istanbul and my hubby had been taking a look at these two rugs for 2 or three days." 2 hours prior to they were going to go to the airport to come back to the US, he went as well as bought the carpets. I asked "just how much did he pay for them?" She stated "42." I said "$ 4200? Well then he did terrific! That's fantastic!!".

She claimed, "no ... he paid $42,000!".

I was surprised! She stated yes, he paid forty-two thousand bucks. I asked her how he paid. When she said American Express, I recognized I can help her. Back then, American Express would certainly take 3 to five days before they would certainly bill a credit score.

I told her she required to call American Express promptly and also have them quit settlement. The carpets her other half purchased were not silke Turkish carpets, as the dealership in Istanbul informed him, they were made in China. I told her also if they were actual Turkish Hereke, there was no chance in the world they would certainly be this price. They would certainly be greater than Chinese carpets, a great deal more, yet nowhere near $42,000. This American couple got ripped off.

Her hubby called American Express to stop the settlement, as well as he called the dealership in Istanbul. In a number of days she came back as well as she asked me to wrap them up so she can deliver them back. I claimed "absolutely!" I covered them as well as she informed me a tale.

She informed me the Istanbul suppliers fell victim to the rate, and also claimed "we'll offer it to you for $10,000, both carpets." She told them, I don't desire it. It's coming back to you and also the repayment's been quit. However despite the fact that this was an experience for her, what was good - she was clever. She made this a finding out experience. She and also her spouse came back in town late at night and after that she concerned me initial thing in the morning. She came in the minute I opened because she needed to know what the carpets deserved. Sure they lost the shipping costs and some time, however this woman was thoughtful and also since she was, she obtained a wonderful lesson without having to pay excessive for it.

A lot of Americans assume if they most likely to a country like Turkey, India, Pakistan - anywhere - they think they're going to obtain a deal due to the fact that they're obtaining a rug from a country resource. But actually it's not a deal, they're paying a lot a lot more. As well as I'll inform you something ... it's an arrangement for vacationers.

The whole point is established for vacationers; from the hotel they're remaining at, to the tourist guide, to the vehicle driver, to the vendor - they all get a share. It's a setup for everybody and also however that's what's going on.

Likewise, here in the united state, if someone markets you a phony rug, you have some recourse as well as you have a chance of recouping your loss.

Exactly how are you going to pursue somebody in a different nation if he offers you a phony carpet? You can not, you simply shed. It's very challenging to purchase well overseas when you don't have the experience that just comes from years of studying these carpets.

In all the years I have actually remained in the carpet business, I have actually only seen someone make an overseas bargain efficiently. He was the Dean of the data division of the College of Louisville. After he retired, he traveled a whole lot, and also he became a collector. He would involve me as well as he started buying rugs and also learning more about rugs. His excitement and also investing a great deal of time in my shop made him a collector. Once, he was traveling in Russia and also he discovered a beautiful carpet which he bought for nothing. I told him he was the only person I have actually ever seen in 40 years who managed a bargain in an international country. People believe they can obtain a good deal on a carpet when they take a trip however it's tricky and also you need to know a whole lot. There's a great deal of factors to utilize a trusted dealer here in your home as opposed to trying to get a bargain overseas.

Maintaining and Caring For Handmade rugs

When you have made the leap into investing in these treasures, you will need to know a few things about how to care for them.

Padding

Something most people don't give much consideration to when they purchase a rug is the rug pad.

This is an essential component of rug possession, commonly overlooked or done on the cheap with devastating repercussions. You've simply invested several thousand bucks for a rug, possibly you're not particular you got a bargain as well as currently the dealer is urging you to acquire what feels like a really expensive pad for this currently expensive rug. It's understandable that a customer would be skeptical. It simply doesn't feel right. However in truth, the a lot more expensive a carpet is, the a lot more it needs an excellent quality pad. Let me describe why ...

We'll reach the security of the carpet momentarily, yet let's begin with the really initial factor correct extra padding is needed, which is the safety of you and also your family members. If you have a hardwood flooring as well as are instantly walking a little faster than normal, the carpet can and also will glide under your feet, sending you crashing to the floor. In 40 years I have seen hands, arms as well as hips damaged as a result of insufficient cushioning. Obtaining a good carpet pad is vital to stop sliding and also secure on your own as well as loved ones from injury.

An additional reason padding is very important is something many people simply don't know if they aren't very educated about rugs. The weight and rubbing of individuals walking on the knots of the carpet is destructive if it touches with the flooring. Knots are knotted around the back of the structure of a carpet, and when there's no padding, in time the knots of a carpet work against the hard floor and also the knots start to degenerate

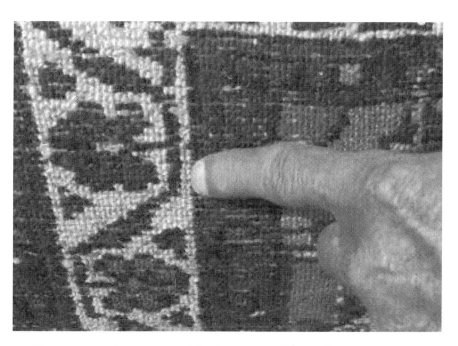

This does not happen overnight, but eventually running the vacuum over the rug, there will start to be hairless areas, due to the fact that there isn't anything left of the back loop of the knot.

Houses with wall to wall carpet also need cushioning for Asian carpets, but also for various factors. Many individuals assume having wall to wall surface rug beneath a rug will certainly function as the pad. However the trouble with an Asian rug in addition to wall surface to wall surface rug is that as you step on them, the rug will certainly begin to move. The rubbing developed in between the carpet and also the carpeting underneath makes the rug change, as well as it can wrinkle or lot up. With time, the carpet will "stroll," that is, action, across the area, bending up against furnishings, and so on. This is not good for the carpet and also is undesirable for your decorating also. A great pad made particularly for this will look after wrinkling as well as "walking" virtually each time.

Lots of people make use of waffle weave gripper extra padding for their carpets, thinking the main reason for cushioning is for its non-slip residential or commercial properties. This type of extra padding is a lot less costly as well as is usually located at large box stores. However, this type of cushioning can do a lot of damage to your carpets and you might not understand the extent of the damages up until it's too late.

The primary reason it's so crucial to make use of good quality solid extra padding is moths. The open area of the waffle weave matting supplies a marvelous breeding place for moths. They enjoy to lay their eggs in the little dark holes, and since it's below the rug, you won't see them till you observe holes in your carpet or moths in your house. In the meanwhile, the moth larvae will certainly have been eating away at your treasured carpet.

Another reason to utilize solid extra padding is that it likewise shields the flooring underneath from spills as well as pet dog urine. With this sort of pad, the liquid (usually red wine) will certainly spread and be absorbed by the pad. If there are openings in the cushioning, the fluid will certainly take a trip downward with to the floor. If you have a child in the house, as an example, and he splashes something, or if a family pet urinates on the rug and you don't know about it, with the strong pad, the fluid can be absorbed as well as there will certainly be little or no damage to the floor below. With a waffle-style pad, the dampness can go unseen on your hardwood flooring, triggering damage that is expensive to fix.

The last reason to have good padding is simply since it behaves to walk on. These rugs are fantastic on your feet and a great pad will certainly make walking on the carpets even more pleasurable. In Iran, for instance, footwear aren't put on inside. While it's customary for people in the United States to put on shoes inside, when you have these attractive carpets as well as have them in your house, it deserves taking your shoes off indoors. There is absolutely nothing like the deluxe of an actual Oriental carpet, especially with a high quality rug pad, under bare feet.

At the end of the day, a good pad isn't cheap, however neither is a great carpet. While it's reasonable somebody could not want to invest another $100-$ 200 after acquiring a numerous thousand buck carpet, but honestly, the much more costly the carpet, the extra it necessitates the defense of an excellent carpet pad. The pad does not need to be transformed yearly. Unless you have a family pet "crash" and also the scent ruins the pad, you can keep it for 15-20 years, so the expense each year computed over the life of the pad truly makes it a bargain contrasted to what you return. Investing in the ideal pad is the right point to do for these beautiful pieces and treating them well will certainly pay you back many.

Maintenance

There are a few things to discuss when maintaining your carpets. I placed these points because group: normal cleaning (vacuuming), rotation, bug avoidance and spot cleaning.

Cleaning up rugs frequently with a vacuum cleaner.

is great and will help the rugs remain nice in between taking them to be professionally cleaned up. One point to be really careful of with a vacuum cleaner is the edges of carpets. The edge is very delicate and also can be damaged by a normal hoover. The damage that can be done by somebody taking the vacuum cleaner to the edge of the rug as well as drawing the edge right into the beater brush is heartbreaking.

Doing this can tear the entire rug apart and when the backing is damaged, oftentimes it's not worth it to repair the rug, so it's effectively ruined.

The way to vacuum an Oriental rug so this never happens is to stop the vacuum's width (usually about a foot) away from the edge of the rug, and then when they are done with the main part of the rug, turn the vacuum 90 degrees and run it along the edge.

Extreme care still needs to be taken to ensure the vacuum *never* goes over the fringe. This is not exaggeration - one careless moment with a vacuum can destroy a rug.

Regular rotation is also very important in caring for these rugs. A general rule of thumb is to rotate rugs every two years. If they are in a high traffic area or in more sunlight, they may require more frequent rotation, perhaps every six months. However often rugs are rotated, consistently doing so will help protect and maintain them.

Moths are destructive little devils, and the enemy of the Oriental carpet owner. They love to go in dark areas. Laying their eggs in low quality padding is just one of their rotten tricks, and there are a lot of other trouble spots. For example, a couch sitting on a rug will be a trouble spot for moths.

Underneath the couch, particularly if it's skirted, is a prime place for moths to hide and lay eggs. Attics and closets, places that people often choose to store unused rugs, are a haven for moths. Everyone has pulled a sweater out of the closet at the first chill of winter and discovered a hole. That's because the closet is warm and dark and the moths have laid eggs there. The eggs grow into larvae and eat the wool threads while they are growing. Once they start to fly off, they have about 21 days to live, and before they die, they find another dark place to lay a new set of eggs.

In dealing with moth problems, the best plan of attack is regular treatment with foggers available at most hardware stores. There are those made especially for moths, and they can be bought fairly inexpensively, sometimes in six packs.

The trick to using these foggers is that three passes are needed. Setting these off around the home, the "fog" will kill the flying moths and some of the larvae, but not all the larvae will be destroyed. It's necessary to wait about two weeks, and then do it again, so any larvae left from the first round that has now developed into a moth will be taken care of.

About two weeks after the second fogging, another application needs to be done. With the third fogging, it is fairly certain that all the moths and their larvae will have been exterminated. However, it's still advisable to be extremely vigilant in looking for new ones. Once there's been an infestation, it's very easy to get them again. Anytime a new hole in a sweater appears and particularly if there are any moths flying around, the fogging method should be applied.

Extreme care should be taken when fogging. Always follow the instructions on the product label, get all the kids and pets out of the house for at least several hours, and cover anything that might come in contact with cooking or eating utensils. Put all food away, ideally in the refrigerator. Wipe all countertops off before putting any food on them. The foggers are effective, but they need to be used properly.

One last thing about moths - they will never eat silk. An absolutely stunning way to moth proof a rug collection, only buy silk rugs. Silk rugs have many advantages, including their beautiful sheen and decadent feel. The drawback of silk rugs, however, is that unlike wool and cotton rugs, silk rugs must never get wet. When silk gets wet, it "crunches" the tip of the fiber which makes it lose its sheen.

Spot cleaning poses one of the biggest challenges for rug owners, especially for people who have children or pets. Do you know what to do if a Coke spills on one of your rugs? Most people think to get a towel and start blotting it. This is actually the worst thing to do; blotting fabric, in this case a rug, pushes the stain down into it. Instead of daubing it up, the stain is becoming more and more embedded in the rug. Instead, a wet/dry shop vac can be used right on the stain to suck as much of the liquid out as possible. Everyone who owns Oriental rugs needs a shop vac. Once the shop vac has gotten as much of the spill out as possible, then take a damp rag and go back and forth over the area of the spill and a little farther than the spill. If the rag picks up stain, rinse it out so that it's clean. This may need to be done several times. Once the stain is out, the last thing to do is wipe the pile of the rug in the right direction while it's still wet, so the nap is lying as it's supposed to. Once the stain is out and the nap is lying correctly, put a fan on the wet area to help it dry. This will take just about any stain out of a rug.

Some harder stains, like red wine, will respond to the same treatment but will need to be flushed as well. After the shop vac has removed as much of the wine as possible and the clean damp rag has removed as much of the stain as possible, the rug needs to be flushed by a specialist. This is tricky because the red wine can't dry, or it will set. Difficult stains, including red wine, pet urine, blood, highly staining fruit juices like pomegranate need to be kept damp until they can be treated. If these substances dry in a rug, they will never come out completely.

If you have the bad luck of a spill late at night and can't get the carpet to the cleaner immediately, once you've vacuumed the stain with the shop vac, use a clean rag to create a small pool of tap water on top of the stain. Once the water has seeped into the rug, use the shop vac again to vacuum the water out. This will help get a bit more of the stain and it should also provide enough moisture to keep the stain from drying until you can take it to your rug cleaner in the morning. I tell my clients that a shop vac is a necessary tool for all Oriental rug collectors.

Professional cleaning

There will be a time when your rugs need to be professionally cleaned. When will depend on where the rugs are located in the house, high traffic vs low traffic. The rug that is placed at the entryway of your home will need to be cleaned every six months. A rug in a formal living room that only gets used at Christmas, on the other hand, can go up to five years before it needs cleaning. The rugs in the family room where you spend most of your time, will need to be cleaned every two to three years.

There are a lot of unscrupulous people who will claim they are professionally cleaning your Oriental rugs when they are not doing so properly. If a rug is cleaned badly, it's worse for the rug, and can do much more damage, than never cleaning it.

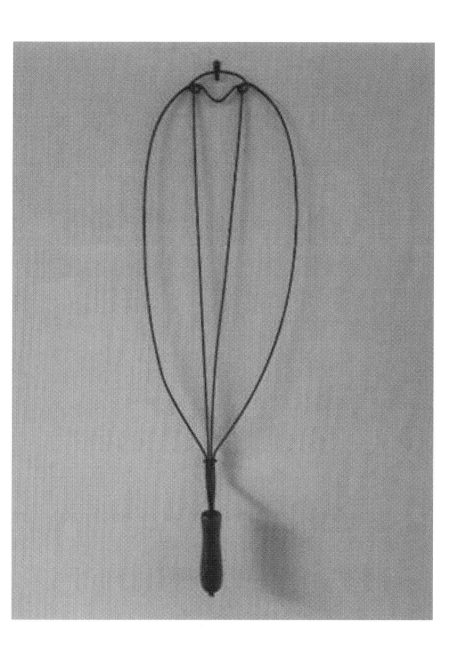

The proper way to clean an Oriental rug begins with dusting it. Many years ago, rugs were beaten to remove sand and other particles. Today, rugs are flipped so the backside is up, and are "beaten" with a commercial vacuum. Half of the vacuum bar is a beater bar made of metal and the other half is a brush. Based on the thickness of the rug, the height of the bar inside the vacuum is adjusted so that it vigorously shakes the rug. This shaking beats all the dirt and particles that are trapped in the pile onto the floor. The process can be time consuming and take up to a half a day for just one rug, and it is the **most important** part of the cleaning.

In fact, if proper dusting isn't done when your rugs are cleaned, it's preferable not to clean them at all. When a rug isn't dusted well, the dirt and grit that is in the rug will be wet down, getting pushed further and further into the pile of the rug, rather than getting cleaned out. Later, as you walk on your rug, that hardened grit that is now deep in the pile acts like little saws, and your footsteps will move this cutting grit back and forth, causing the pile to wear away, eventually doing great damage to the rug. Dusting the rug is a critical step in maintaining it.

Once the rug is fully dusted, with no more dirt coming out of it, the rug is flipped back over topside up and is vacuumed thoroughly, ensuring all the grit is removed. Then the rug is washed. This next step is also critical. I've seen couples get divorced over bad washing. Not just once but twice. Instead of having a rug professionally cleaned, one of the couple decides to take the rug out on the driveway and hose it down. When the colors bleed, the rug - and the marriage - is ruined.

Before washing the rug, the colors are tested to determine how color fast they are. Next, the rug will be wet down depending on how fast the dyes are. In some rugs the dyes are very well set and the rug can be completely soaked with water. Other rugs require much more care and will need to be delicately dampened. A note here; only cool water is ever used in a proper rug washing. Heat, particularly steam, is one of the most expedient ways to ruin a rug. Hot water will dissolve the dye. As mentioned earlier, the yarns are boiled with dye which sets it, and using hot water, especially steam, reverses that process, unsetting the dye and making it run.

With the rug as wet as it can be, it's then gently scrubbed. At our shop we use a detergent that is so mild that it is the only one used on museum pieces. The rug should be scrubbed with a hand brush only. Once that is done, the rug is rinsed, and in most cases, suction will be used to get the rinse water out of the rug. At this point, the rug isn't wet anymore, just damp. Then the rugs are dried flat, not hung. Even on a rug with very good color set, the dyes can still run ever so slightly and gravity will pull those colors out when a rug is hung, a risk that's not worth taking. Lastly, while the rug is still damp, a special pile brush is used to bring all the pile in the correct direction. Once that's done, the rug is left to dry, usually with a fan with a bit of heat. The entire process takes about three to five days. If you take your rug in to be cleaned and they give it back to you the next day, it has not been cleaned properly.

Right after a professional cleaning is a great time to rotate a rug. Regular rotation will expose a rug evenly to sunlight and wear. If you keep your rugs on a regular cleaning schedule, they will also be on a regular rotational schedule, which will help maintain their durability and beauty. A great thing to know about rugs to help remember which side needs to be turned; every rug has a "dark" side and a "light" side. Standing at the finishing end, the rug will look lighter and standing at the "bottom" of a rug, it will look darker. It's a fun thing to walk from one end to the other as the difference can be very dramatic. But it's also quite practical to know this because, taking note of which end is where when the rug was sent to be cleaned, you will know which way to orient the rug when it comes back.

Storage

When storing a rug, it should be fully cleaned and when taking it in, tell the cleaner it's going to be packed up for storage. Next, take moth balls or moth flakes and put them in old socks. As the rug is rolled up, the socks with the moth repellant go into the rolled rug. The cleaner can do this as well.

Once the rug is rolled, the outside of the rolled rug should be rolled with brown paper. This is a very important step as it will help absorb any moisture that gets in and could potentially damage the warp threads if they are cotton, or worse yet, silk. Lastly, the rolled, paper wrapped rug gets wrapped in plastic and sealed. A rug can be kept like this for 10 years or more and as long as the plastic isn't damaged, the rug will be like it was when it was put away.

When taking rugs out of storage, they will need to be aired because they will smell strongly of moth repellent. Vacuuming the rug and allowing it to air out, the smell will go away and the rug is ready to be enjoyed again. Good, proper storage is very important. Rugs that are stored poorly can suffer moisture and of course moth damage that cannot be repaired. When in doubt about storage, a professional cleaner is the way to go. It will save a lot of heartbreak when it comes time to unroll a favorite stored rug.

Protecting your collection

There are a number of things you can do to help protect your rug collection. First is choosing the right rug for the right place in your home.

One mistake many people make is putting an inexpensive rug in a high traffic area. This is absolutely not the thing to do. At first blush the thinking is understandable, but upon closer examination, it becomes clear why this is a bad idea.

There are rugs - for example Baluch rugs from Afghanistan - that are extremely tough. They are so well constructed and are designed for heavy traffic. They can be walked on all day long, every day, and will continue to look incredible for 100 years.

It's an expensive rug, but it's a dense rug and it's made to be used, particularly in a high traffic area. An inexpensive rug won't be durable and will have to be replaced in a few years, as it just cannot withstand the abuse. If constrained by budget, choose a few more well made expensive pieces to put in high traffic areas. Put less expensive rugs in lower traffic areas for the opposite reason; a lower traffic area will mean less wear and tear on the rug, and something of lower quality construction will be fine there. Matching the right rug for the area you're decorating is extremely important to the life of the rug.

Another common mistake is using a small rug as a bathmat. This can be done, but choose with care. If the rug's weft is made of cotton, it will deteriorate quickly if it doesn't dry well. It's much better to use a wool weft rug because wool is more water repellant and dries fast, so it will last longer if it gets a little wet.

When putting a rug under a sofa, as mentioned before, moths will be problematic. Choosing a cotton weft rug for that area, even if there is a moth problem, will ensure they don't eat the weft, which makes the rug easier to repair if there is damage.

Kilim rugs are beautiful and have a special place in the hearts of many collectors. Most people don't know this, but kilims are not made to be floor rugs; they are made to be decorative for the walls or sometimes a covering for the opening of a tent. They are too delicate to walk on all the time. When putting a kilim on the floor, it should be located in a place where no one ever walks, especially not pets with claws. Kilims make beautiful wall and ceiling decorations and are better suited to be used this way than as floor coverings.

Sunlight is an interesting problem. Oriental rugs are meant to be used, and seen, not to be hidden away in the dark. But the sun is going to fade a rug, no two ways about that. Proper rotation will serve your rugs well, in that rotating will fade a rug evenly and actually can give a beautiful look to your rugs.

Sometimes a rug gets very strong exposure to sunlight and can fade dramatically. I have some clients who once put a rug in such strong sunlight that it almost ruined the rug. This rug was put in a room facing a window with full sun in Arizona.

When they sent it to me, it was essentially one solid color, it was so bleached. We were able to rescue the rug by shearing it.

Because the sun had just bleached the very tip of the wool yarns, we were able to take the shearers and remove the faded part.

When a rug is going to have this kind of UV exposure, the best thing to do is cover the windows with a clear UV blocking film, which will block out 99% of the UV. Even in full sun with the curtains open, the rug will be immune to fading.

Another thing that is often not considered during day to day use of rugs is the delicate part, no matter how durable they are. The edge of a rug, whether it's the side edge or the fringe edge, is the most vulnerable to damage by foot traffic. Every time someone steps on it, it wears it out a little more.

These delicate parts can also be damaged just because people don't understand what they are doing. For example, when a housekeeper comes to clean the floors and doesn't fold the rugs back while mopping, the chemicals in the floor cleaner will start to fade and eat away at the edges of the rug.

While it's virtually impossible to ensure the edges of rugs are never touched, either by people or chemicals, and of course pets, with a little care, it is possible to be mindful enough to safeguard rugs. Of course, every visitor who comes to the house should not be ordered to take off their shoes and watch the edges of the rugs - that is the opposite of hospitality. But as owners we can be mindful about how we walk, set a good example for our children and coach them, as well as teaching anyone who regularly comes into the house how to care for the rugs. Walking on a rug carefully is a simple and easy thing to do, as is being mindful of using chemical cleaners. Young kids often think that walking on rugs without stepping on the edges is a fun game!

The last thing on this delicate subject; when living with a rug, this kind of damage is virtually invisible because it's so slow and gradual. Suddenly an edge will look a little worn, which is a real problem. By the time damage is visible to the naked eye, it can deteriorate rapidly and needs to be attended by a professional who can repair it.

These rugs are made to last a long time, but they have to be taken care of, both before and after "problems' arise.

Restoration

Sometimes things just happen and rugs must be repaired and restored. When damage is severe, it's best to take the rug to an experienced repairman. At Sara's Oriental Rugs, we are trained in rugmaking and can do expert repairs, as well as can be done in an original rug making country. If a dealer doesn't do repairs themselves at their shop, they should be able to recommend someone.

There are different levels of damage a rug can suffer. A rug where the pile is completely worn away will sometimes have marker coloring the bald spot (this sounds crazy, but it's true). This is called a "painted" rug, and can sometimes be fixed to restore the value, particularly if the weft is intact. However, when buying a rug like this, a savvy collector will not pay full price. A discount, at least commensurate with the cost of the repair, should be given. When unsure how much that is, ask to "try" the rug at home and take it to a repairperson. Whatever the cost of the repair is the minimum discount that you should receive.

An unevenly worn rug can be fixed, and is almost always worth fixing, if the rug still has some pile left on it. The entire rug can be sheared to bring the pile to an even point. This requires a lot of skill and not shearing a rug properly can completely ruin the rug, so the person doing this must be well trained in how to do it.

A rug that has a foundation problem, where the warp is damaged, whether from rotting or from moths or even just a tear through, can be fixed in two different ways. A dealer will be able to look at a rug that is damaged and advise a client how best to approach the repair. One way is to rebuild the foundation, which is very expensive and rarely worth the cost in comparison to the actual value of the rug. Unless a rug has sentimental value, if it costs more to do a full restoration than the rug is worth, a good dealer will not advise the restoration. The right handmade rugs from the right areas will always go up in value, but once you put into a rug more than it's worth, you won't have an appreciating asset. You just have a rug.

The other way is to patch the rug with another piece of rug. All rug repair shops will have spare pieces of carpets that can be cut and matched, reasonably well, to the carpet that needs to be fixed. The patch is sewn into the carpet and will stop the hole from growing.

This kind of patch will definitely keep the problem from getting worse, which is important. But it does not restore the value of the rug. Nothing except rebuilding the foundation and the pile will restore the value. This is the **key** reason that taking good care of these rugs is so important; treating them as an asset and seeing them appreciate, requires that they are well maintained. It's not difficult to do, but there is no real margin for error. Once the rug is torn through or worn to the point that there is no pile, restoring its value is virtually impossible. A little bit of care pays off immensely here.

Often when a rug is not worth fully restoring, but is still a lovely rug, it will be worth repairing to the point that it does not suffer more damage. If, for example, the edge is frayed and the weft is damaged, instead of restoring the rug, it can be bound along that edge to stop additional fraying and the rug can still be enjoyed. Again, a good relationship with a dealer is critical to helping make these decisions. He or she will be able to help evaluate the rug and determine the best course of action.

Valuing and protecting your collection

Collectors enjoy knowing the value of their possessions, particularly those who expect the value of their collections to go up. And once they know the value of their collection, they generally want protection for that collection, which leads us to the topics of appraisal and insurance.

Appraising your collection

There are different reasons to have an appraisal done, and there are different kinds of appraisals.Taking a look at these will help understand when and how to use appraisers.

The first kind of appraisal is a casual appraisal. It's been reiterated several times here the need to build a trusting relationship with a good dealer. A serious collector realizes that this relationship is the most important tool in creating a collection. A trusted dealer can be the first "appraisal" for a potential rug. This kind of dealer will do two things; their rugs will be fairly priced and they will give you an honest opinion on the price of a rug from another dealer. In addition to allowing clients to take rugs home to see how they fit in a space, a good dealer you buy from regularly will give an opinion of any rug's value, free of charge. At Sara's Oriental Rugs we will always give a professional opinion to any client, as the correct market retail price of a rug, no matter where the rug comes from.

Another kind of appraisal is the kind done for insurance purposes. This kind of appraisal will involve a report done by a certified appraiser, which will detail numerous things about the rug, including country of origin, age or estimated age, construction, weave, pattern, damage and many other things.

All of this information is interesting and can be valuable to the owner of the rug, but the most important part of the report is the appraised retail value of the rug. Proper insurance will cover this retail value if anything happens to the rug, flood, fire, theft, etc. This kind of appraisal is usually a paid service, and likely can be done by your regular dealer.

Another instance an "official" appraisal might be needed is during the liquidation of an estate. When there are many heirs to an estate, sometimes one or more heirs will want the rugs in the estate. Just as a house in an estate is appraised to split the value between heirs, valuable rugs will be appraised in the same way.

Yet another kind of appraisal that can be done is for your own inventory to value your collection for yourself and be able to add a numeric value to your net worth statement. This might be done in a few ways. If reflecting as large an amount as possible on your personal balance sheet is the goal, an insurance type of appraisal done on all your rugs and using that full retail price to value your collection will be the way to go. If on the other hand you are looking to realistically assess what you own - or in other words, what your rugs might actually bring if you sell them - the more casual kind of appraisal would work better, as it will produce a lower, more realistic market price for your rugs. Again, this underscores the importance of having a good relationship with a dealer. Often a dealer will do this for you for no charge, particularly if you are regularly buying and exchanging rugs. Most dealers who love what they do are happy to "talk shop" about the market and how rugs are selling at any given time. Most will be delighted to let you know what they think your rugs will sell for, especially if they are the dealer who sold it to you.

Another option for this kind of valuation is to simply decide on a percentage off of the retail valuation from the official insurance appraisal. Again, you are going to need the guidance of a good dealer, and it would be helpful if this dealer is the same one who does the insurance appraisal.

Insuring your collection

Insurance is generally not everyone's favorite topic, but as you grow as a collector of any valuable item, it becomes more and more important to understand. Most of us regard insurance as an annoyance, something we should do, but fundamentally don't want to. Much like a regular dentist appointment, the purpose of which is to spend a little time and effort now to avoid a cavity or root canal, insurance for rugs protects a collection from the unknown possible problems of the future. Let's take a brief look at insurance and how it works.

Today, there are a few ways to go about insuring a valuable rug collection. If there are only a few rugs in the collection, a rider can be added to a current homeowners policy. The insurance company will ask that the rugs be specifically listed, described (usually just a style and size is needed) and valued. Full retail price can be used for the replacement cost. Listing rugs specifically like this on a homeowner's policy will cover up to certain value amounts (determined by the policy) and cause the policy premium to increase.

Collections that are very large or include very valuable rugs may require a "Valuable Items" Coverage policy. This type of policy will also list out each of the rugs in a collection (or "schedule" them), but will have much higher replacement value limits. An example of a rug that would likely require this kind of coverage is a large antique sarpi. These rugs are often valued at over $20,000 a piece, and the limit of a homeowners policy can often be $10,000 or even less. While adding a rider might not require an appraisal, this type of policy, particularly with high value rugs, almost certainly will. And it's worth the cost for the peace of mind. The last thing any collector wants is the heartbreak of losing a piece and finding out that it was likely more valuable than originally thought.

An important thing to consider when shopping around for insurance for rugs is exclusions. Many policyholders do not fully understand what is and what is not covered in their policies, and it's worth a bit of time to have a conversation with an insurance agent to discover where there might be any lack of coverage, known as a "gap" in the insurance world, in your own policy. And these gaps are not always obvious or immediately evident. Covering these gaps in an insurance policy is not difficult, but one needs to be aware of them. A good insurance broker will take the time to talk to you about your collection and find the coverage you want. While no one likes to pay for things they hope will not happen, the best advice is to get quality insurance with a carrier known for easy claims. It's worth the extra premium.

Made in the USA
Coppell, TX
09 February 2022

73271032R00053